GREAT LEAPS FORWARD

Modernizers in Africa, Asia, and Latin America

Cyrus Veeser
Bentley University

D0037281

Prentice Hall

Boston   Columbus   Indianapolis   New York   San Francisco
Upper Saddle River   Amsterdam   Cape Town   Dubai   London   Madrid
Milan   Munich   Paris   Montreal   Toronto   Delhi   Mexico City
Sao Paulo   Sydney   Hong Kong   Seoul   Singapore   Taipei   Tokyo

Editorial Director: Leah Jewell
Executive Editor: Charles Cavaliere
Editorial Assistant: Lauren Aylward
Director of Marketing:
  Brandy Dawson
Senior Marketing Manager: Maureen Prado
  Roberts
Production Manager: Kathy Sleys
Creative Director: Jayne Conte
Cover Designer: Bruce Kenselaar
Manager, Visual Research: Beth Brenzel
Manager, Rights and Permissions:
  Zina Arabia

Image Permission Coordinator:
  Annette Linder
Manager, Cover Visual Research &
Permissions: Karen Sanatar
Cover Art: Stock certificate, *Chemins de Fer Ethiopiens*, collection of the author
Maps: Alliance Publishing
Full-Service Project Management:
  Sadagoban Balaji
Composition: Integra Software Services, Ltd

Text Font: 11/13 Palatino

Credits and acknowledgments borrowed from other sources and reproduced, with permission, in this textbook appear on appropriate page within text.

Library of Congress Cataloging-in-Publication Data

Veeser, Cyrus.
  Great leaps forward : modernizers in Africa, Asia, and Latin America/Cyrus Veeser.
    p. cm.—(Connections)
  Includes bibliographical references and index.
  ISBN-13: 978-0-13-199848-3
  ISBN-10: 0-13-199848-X
    1. Statesmen--Biography.   2. Díaz Porfirio, 1830–1915.   3. Menelik II, Negus of Ethiopia, 1844–1913.   4. Sun, Yat-sen, 1866–1925.   5. Atatürk, Kemal, 1881–1938.   6. History, Modern.
I. Title.
D412.6.V44 2010
321.0092'2—dc22

                                                                                    2009027939

Prentice Hall
is an imprint of

www.pearsonhighered.com

ISBN 10:   0-13-199848-X
ISBN 13: 978-0-13-199848-3

Contents

3   SUN YATSEN: REVOLUTIONARY OUTSIDER   89

4   MUSTAFA KEMAL: MUSLIM MODERNITY   122

Foreword

Connections: Key Themes in World History focuses on specific issues of world historical significance from antiquity to the present by employing a combination of explanatory narrative, primary sources, questions relating to those sources, a summary analysis ("Making Connections"), and further points to ponder, all of which combine to enable readers to discover some of the most important driving forces in world history. The increasingly rapid pace and specialization of historical inquiry has created an ever-widening gap between professional publications and general surveys, especially surveys of world history. The purpose of *Connections* is to bridge that gap by placing the latest research and debates on selected topics of global historical significance, as well as some of the evidence upon which historians base their insights, into a form and context that is comprehensible to students and general readers alike.

Two pedagogical principles infuse this series. First, students master world history most easily if allowed to focus on specific themes and issues. Such themes, by their very specificity, as well as because of their general application, enable students to perceive and understand the overall patterns and meaning of our shared global past more clearly than is possible through reading, by itself, a massive world history textbook. Second, students learn best when asked to think critically about what they are studying. So far as the study of history is concerned, critical thinking necessarily involves analysis of primary sources.

To that end, we offer a series of brief, tightly focused books that embrace a radical simplicity and a provocative format. Each book goes to the heart of a key theme, phenomenon, or issue in world history—something that has connected humans across cultures, continents, and time spans. By actively engaging with this material, the reader comes to understand in a nuanced and meaningful manner how often distantly located human cultures have been connected to one another as key actors in the epic story of world history.

Alfred J. Andrea
Series Editor
Professor Emeritus of History
University of Vermont

Series Editor's Preface

Statues and photos of Mustafa Kemal Atatürk in European civilian clothes and Turkish military dress are to be seen everywhere throughout the Republic of Turkey. One of my favorites, encountered in a little town in Cappadocia, deep in the heart of southeastern Anatolia, shows him in formal evening attire and opera cape, a reminder not only of his love of Western classical music but, more importantly, his patronage of a new art form, Turkish national opera, which married indigenous folk music and Western polyphony. Consequently, when I stepped onto the main campus of Istanbul University on April 16, 2009, I was not surprised to see multiple images of the Father of the Turks gracing the university's halls and grounds. What I did not expect was a heroic statue of him dressed in a Roman toga. But upon reflection, that statue, in which Atatürk is flanked by two similarly heroic, Greco-Roman-like figures—a strong, athletic young woman bearing a lighted torch and a muscular young man carrying the republic's flag—fittingly reflects in its symbols the objectives and methods that he pursued in bringing the Turks into the modern world and crafting their republic. It also speaks to his level of success,

Statue of Atatürk in a toga, Istanbul University

inasmuch as this, the first modern university in Turkey, is home today to about 70,000 women and men who pursue a wide variety of studies in the humanities, sciences, social sciences, and a number of professional fields.

As an integral part of transforming the new nation of Turkey into a secular, modern state based on Western republican principles, Atatürk instituted a number of educational reforms, including a total reorganization in 1933 of Istanbul Darülfünum (Istanbul House of Multiple Sciences), a school devoted largely to the applied sciences and founded in 1846. Believing that the Darülfünum inadequately prepared students for leadership in the new Turkey and their place in the world, he transformed it into Istanbul University, the first modern, Western-style university in Turkey. Many others followed.

The toga worn by Atatürk in this statue places him, therefore, in the pantheon of classical Western educational leaders stretching back over two millennia—educators, at least in the opinion of those responsible for this statue, whose furtherance of learning had underpinned Europe's vitality. It also underscores the fact that, in the minds of those who promoted it, modernization in Turkey included learning the ways and wisdom of the West, while remaining proudly Turkish. The symbolic meaning of the youths whom Atatürk is guiding and encouraging, one bearing a token of enlightenment and progress and the other the banner of national unity and each exemplifying the classical Western ideal of *mens sana in corpore sano* (sound mind in a sound body), is so obvious that it needs no further exegesis.

Likewise, memorials to the memory of Sun Yatsen abound wherever substantial bodies of Chinese are to be found, regardless of their political loyalties and ideologies. Often known as Zhongshan Parks, they include a former imperial pleasure garden in Beijing close by Tiananmen Square, the political heart of the People's Republic of China (PRC). On any day, thousands of citizens of the PRC visit it to pay their respects. The same is true of his final resting place, but even more so. Although built by the Guomindang government soon after his death in 1925, in a style that joined traditional imperial tomb architecture and modern forms, the massive mausoleum of this Father of Modern China at Zijinshan (Purple Mountain) just outside Nanjing, remains a site revered, protected, and promoted as a place of secular pilgrimage and veneration by the PRC. The PRC has not even seen fit to replace the mosaic flag of the Guomindang that graces the ceiling. When the Guomindang were defeated in 1949 and moved their seat of government to Taiwan, they brought the civic cult of Sun Yatsen with them. Chief of his many memorials there is the National Dr. Sun Yatsen Memorial Hall in Taipei City, which rivals the awe-inspiring Sun Yatsen Memorial Hall in Guangzhou (Canton), where this revolutionary physician had established a military government in 1921. In like fashion, diaspora Chinese overseas continue to revere his memory. One of their most beautiful memorials to him is the classical Chinese scholar's garden in Vancouver, British Columbia.

Less pervasive and widespread, but no less sincerely offered, are Ethiopia's memorials to its great modernizer, Emperor Menelik II. In the heart of the capital of Addis Ababa, a city Menelik founded in 1887, stands a great square named for him, featuring his equestrian statue erected by Emperor Haile Selassie in 1930. Such is the hold that Menelik II has on Ethiopia's national memory, this statue was one of the few imperial monuments to survive the Marxist Revolution of 1974–1987.

In like fashion, the mausoleum housing his remains and those of Empress Taytu, his wife, escaped profanation. Moreover, the Battle of Adowa (Adwa), in which Menelik's forces defeated an invading Italian army in 1896, has been the proud subject of countless Ethiopian paintings for the past century and more, and has also been a focal point of much Ethiopian literature and music. Indeed, many non-Ethiopian pan-Africanists at home and abroad have likewise celebrated that victory in their art and political rhetoric.

And so we have three great modernizers who appear in this marvelous little book crafted by Cyrus Veeser, each of whom is to this day a living presence in his native land and among his people, although their respective deaths were 1938, 1925, and 1913. But this book also covers the career of a fourth modernizer, Porfirio Díaz, for whom there are no memorials along the avenues of modern Mexico or in the hearts of his countrymen today. Following his ouster from power in 1911, Mexico was plunged into a bloody, protracted revolution. It was his sad destiny to live to see the first four years of that bitter, tragic struggle. The career of Díaz, therefore, serves as a corrective for those who would see the work of late 19th- and early 20th-century modernization as one of unalloyed success. Moreover, thanks to Veeser's carefully nuanced study, the reader is able to perceive the strengths and weaknesses, the successes and failures of each of these four leaders. In essence, through a careful reading of this book we learn not only how but also how far and to what effect they prodded their nations and people to "great leaps forward."

Alfred J. Andrea
Series Editor

About the Author

Cyrus Veeser earned his Ph.D. in history at Columbia University, where his dissertation won the Bancroft prize. He has been a Fulbright and NEH fellow, as well as a fellow at Harvard University's Charles Warren Center. He is currently associate professor of history at Bentley University in Waltham, Massachusetts.

Acknowledgments

The idea for this book came long before its realization. Along the way, many people helped the project take shape, including Frank Scretchings, Anders Stephanson, Carol Gluck, Eric Foner, Barbara Fields, Norman Finkelstein, Emelio Betances, the late Faruk Tabak, Iftikhar Ahmad, Adele Oltman, Marc Stern, Bob Hannigan, and Ariel Salzmann.

The turning point came when Charles Cavaliere, Pearson's crackerjack world history executive editor, looked across a coffee table in the lounge outside Bentley's history department and said something to the effect of, "Let's do it!" Through the many discussions of title, subtitle, maps, photographs, and content that followed, Charles never lost his initial enthusiasm, for which I thank him heartily. Thanks also to Lauren Aylward and Bruce Kenselaar at Pearson and to Bentley University for supporting this and other research projects.

All readers of *Great Leaps Forward* owe a debt of gratitude to Al Andrea, general editor of the Connections series and world historian extraordinaire, for his tireless, painstaking care with the manuscript. I had no idea series editors worked so hard! Al enforced a scrupulous adherence to accuracy with his encyclopedic knowledge of events on several continents. Since he is infallible, all remaining errors in this book are most certainly my own.

For careful reading of chapters in manuscript and gentle suggestions for improvement, my thanks to Fahri Basegmez, H. Aram Veeser, Gaynor Ellis, Bridie Minehan, and Lilian Bobea, as well as reviewers Rick Warner, Wabash College, and Hayrettin Yucesoy, St. Louis University. For help with translations and all-around support, I owe a debt of gratitude to Paqui Revert and Gervais Morin in Valencia, Spain.

This book is dedicated to Lilian, Gabriela, and Minerva.

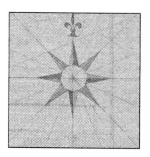

Introduction

In the spirit of the *Connections* series, the book in your hands focuses on one large theme that connects many events in our shared global experience. The theme is simple enough: that the extraordinary rise to power of "the West"—meaning Western Europe first and later the United States—forced less-developed nations across the planet to try to catch up. Half of the story—the rise of the West—has been told often and well. The other half—how less-developed parts of the world understood and responded to the vast new power of the West—has rarely been told in a systematic and comparative way. That is the goal of this book.

Getting a new perspective on what William McNeill famously called "the Rise of the West" is not easy, especially for anyone who grew up in the United States.[1] Americans tend to see their history as an unstoppable rise to world leadership. Imagine for a moment a U.S. history course compressed into a 60-second video: feisty Americans win independence, spread democracy to the Pacific, end slavery, build the world's leading industrial economy, win two world wars, embrace equal rights for all, defeat Communism, and invent the Internet. Success and progress shine through every moment of the story.

It is difficult for us living in the West to visualize how "our" rise to power looked to, and changed, societies in places as distant and different as China, Mexico, Ethiopia, and Turkey. To understand the world we live in, however, it is useful to think about how "the Rise of the West" hurt or helped, angered or inspired, excluded or included the rest of the world. The fact is, today as in 1900, most people in the world live in countries that resemble China, Mexico, and Turkey more than they do the United States or England.

DEFINITIONS

The West and "the Rest," then, is our theme, but with a twist. The West will remain, for the most part, offstage, while the starring roles go to four nonindustrial nations and their dramatic struggles to modernize. Let's begin with a few definitions.

When this book uses the shorthand term *the West*, it is referring to the world's major military–industrial powers, above all Britain and France from 1800 on, joined by Germany and the United States after 1850. Lesser European powers, including Italy, Belgium, the Netherlands, Russia, Spain, and Portugal, were also part of the West. By the early 1900s, one Asian nation, Japan, had modernized its economy and military enough to be considered a Great Power, though it did not quite join the club of the West.

A second important point is that the rise of the West was not merely a question of military might. The growing power of the West took many forms. *Power* does not just mean the machine guns, long-range cannon, and steel-hulled battleships that Europe and the United States built after 1850, important though they were. Power also means the development of machine-driven factories that poured out cloth, tools, and other products by the mid-1800s in the most developed countries. Our definition of power also includes the rapid accumulation of capital—money—in European and American banks. Much of that money was invested in the developing world and became a key point of encounter between the West and the Rest. Political changes also made the West more powerful. Governments in Europe and the United States became more democratic (at least until the rise of Fascism in the 1920s), creating a solid political base for the growing wealth, industry, and technology of the West.

Knowledge was another pillar of Western power. By 1900, the West had a near monopoly on the production and transmission of information. Europe and the United States printed 90 percent of the world's newspapers and most of the world's books. In 1900, the United States alone had 977 colleges and universities. The entire continent of Africa had just five colleges in 1900—two ancient Islamic schools in Egypt and Morocco and three modern colleges in Liberia and Sierra Leone. In imperial China, with a population of over 400 million, higher education was limited to academies that drilled students on classic Confucian texts to prepare them for government service, apart from a handful of colleges opened by Christian missionaries after 1840. The concentration of universities, newspapers, and books in a handful of industrialized countries ensured that Western thought would dominate the world. The West's ideas about science, economics, education, government, religious liberty, and women's rights—among other topics—profoundly influenced the thinking of nationalist leaders in the periphery.

Two kindred terms also need definition—*modernity* and *modernization*. The dictionary tells us that "modernity" means something that is "of the present" or recent past. That's how we normally use the term—modern as opposed to old-fashioned. But for historians (and now for you) modernity doesn't just mean new or up-to-date. Instead the term signals a particular kind of society that only came into existence over the past 200 years or so, first in Western Europe, then elsewhere. "Modernization" refers to a society that is moving toward modernity, a circular definition that will have to do for now.

Earlier theories of modernization emphasized the *sameness* of modern societies—what they all had in common, and what made them different from premodern societies. Despite some nuances, these earlier ideas assumed that modernization was in fact Westernization, with developing societies approximating, insofar as possible, the economic, political, intellectual, social, and even religious structures of Western Europe and the United States. The essential features of modernity, in the older views, included "urbanization, widespread literacy, a high degree of usage of inanimate power, rising per capita income, [and] the widespread participation of the populace in political affairs," along with more abstract qualities such as the West's rational, secular, and scientific orientations toward the world.[2]

Historians now understand that modernity is plural, not singular. Modernizing societies retain much of their own culture, reshaping foreign ideas and institutions to fit their needs, and thereby creating hybrid societies. Thus modernization cannot be reduced to "a simple replication of Western experiences."[3] Even if it could, which Western experiences are we talking about? Does modernity mean building a powerful navy or nurturing a multiparty democracy? Guaranteeing equal rights for women or implementing a eugenic program of sterilization for epileptics and the blind? Nonindustrial nations aspired to have steel mills and textile factories—but did they also want the volatile working class that tended the machinery? Large cities symbolized modernity, but what about the criminals, prostitutes, beggars, and drunks that inhabited them? Modernity demanded more schools and new universities, yet students often spearheaded demonstrations against their own governments.

It seems that modernity has a bewildering array of contradictory meanings—heavy industry and literacy, representative democracy and the latest artillery, electrified cities and the angry unemployed. Porfirio Díaz wanted a modern Mexico just as Mustafa Kemal wanted a modern Turkey, but the societies they envisioned were far from identical. The meaning of modernity varies not only from country to country and era to era, but even within a single country at one moment in time. No single definition of modernity or modernization will suffice, but the terms will take on layers of meaning as you read about the changes pursued by modernizers in Africa, Asia, and Latin America.

One final definition—the *periphery*. In the 1800s, Europeans compared their "civilized world," or Christendom, with the "uncivilized world" of the heathen, "our little brown brothers" across the ocean, as William Howard Taft famously called Filipinos. Today we use nicer terms: the Third World, the developing world, less-developed countries, or the periphery. For our purposes, the periphery does not necessarily mean countries that are not Christian. Latin America, which is overwhelmingly Roman Catholic, is clearly part of the developing world. Here, the periphery means all the countries that before the mid-20th century had a large percentage of their people engaged in subsistence agriculture, lacked powerful armies and large-scale industry, and failed to create stable democratic governments. The periphery also included the great swath of European colonies spreading from Jamaica in the Caribbean to the Philippines in the Pacific.

These "peripheral" countries and colonies in fact contained about four-fifths of the world's population in 1800.

THE WEST INVENTS MODERNITY

Industry, technology, weaponry, money, knowledge—all these elements of power came together to make the West a new phenomenon in world history. In 1400, by many measures, China was the most advanced nation in the world. A rational observer at that time would have bet that China, not England, would dominate the world in 1900. Rapid changes in the West, however, reversed the relative superiority of China.

By 1900, the industrialized West had become radically different from the still rural, still agrarian areas of Asia, Africa, the Middle East, and Latin America. And here's a key point: It was the West that was abnormal. The rest of the world was moving in step with the slow progress of human development since the discovery of agriculture roughly 10,000 years ago. Western Europe and the United States broke the mold. In the 1930s, just three countries—Britain, Germany, and the United States—supplied roughly two-thirds of the world's industrial goods. Factory workers, the backbone of the industrial world, made up only 4 percent of the world's population just before World War II. This small group of industrialized nations was so disproportionately powerful, however, that they changed the course of world history. Both World War I and World War II were struggles among this handful of nations, even though the battlegrounds spilled over into less-developed regions.

How was it possible for Europe, relatively backward before 1400, to leap ahead of Asia by 1800? To understand that, we need to step back for a moment and take a long view of human development. Since *Homo sapiens*, or modern humans, evolved over 150,000 years ago, there have been two decisive turning points in our history. The first, the invention of agriculture some 10,000 years ago, allowed humans to give up the wandering lives of hunter-gatherers and settle in farming communities. Knowledge of agriculture gradually spread, and eventually the vast majority of human beings lived out their lives as farmers. Yes, there were princes and priestesses, goldsmiths and potters, but most people, whether in China or South America, West Africa or the Euphrates Valley, coaxed a living from the Earth. It makes sense, then, that the Hebrew Bible places the imperative to farm at the dawn of human history. "With labor you shall win your food from [the soil] all the days of your life," God declares as he expels Adam and Eve from Eden in the book of Genesis.

The second great leap in human history happened a little more than 200 years ago, with a set of changes we call the Industrial Revolution. This breakthrough happened first in England in the late 1700s. The use of steam engines, power looms, and the factory system initially changed the way that cotton and wool cloth was made. Slow, labor-intensive spinning wheels and handlooms became obsolete as yarn and cloth streamed from England's new textile factories, the "dark Satanic mills" of William Blake's famous poem. In essence, the Industrial Revolution transferred human labor and skill to machines powered first by water, then by steam, and after 1900 by electricity. Because factories increased production, skilled workers and inventors soon adapted them to make tools, guns, pots and pans, clocks, and other basic consumer goods. Factory-made products cost much less than handmade goods and relentlessly undermined artisan production. Professions that had existed for thousands of years— the skilled handcrafts of weavers, blacksmiths, coopers, cobblers, potters—became obsolete and nearly vanished within a generation or two. Over the course of the 19th century, manufacturing spread to continental Europe, the United States, and eventually Japan.

WAS THERE AN INDUSTRIAL REVOLUTION?

This book is not about the Industrial Revolution in Europe, but since we will look closely at the efforts of modernizers outside Europe to catch up with the industrial powers, it is important to understand the complex series of changes we call the Industrial Revolution.

By using the term Industrial *Revolution*, we are tacitly accepting two controversial ideas. The first is that the industrial breakthrough was sudden, and the second is that it signaled a sharp rupture with what came before it. For decades historians and economists took both of those ideas for granted. More recently, many have insisted that there was no "leap" in the output of goods that justifies using the term *revolution*. Rather than being a dramatic break with the past, the so-called Industrial Revolution was "the culmination of a most unspectacular process, the consequence of a long period of slow economic growth."[4] These historians emphasize continuity with the past and minimize the importance of "decisive innovations" like the spinning jenny or water frame as triggers of industrial growth.

It is now clear that the Industrial Revolution was not simply the result of a few technological breakthroughs. If a handful of inventions had really triggered the Industrial Revolution, less-developed nations could have modernized simply by importing the new technology from Great Britain. As we shall see, nationalist leaders in Asia, Africa, and Latin America learned that catching up with the West was not so simple. In the few countries where it happened, the Industrial Revolution erupted out of deeper social changes—changes that allowed farmers to produce more food, encouraged the building of better roads, led to improvements in literacy, and pushed investment into new ventures by giving legal protection to private property. This centuries-long lead up to industrialization helps explain why the leap to modernity happened first in Britain and Western Europe. In other words, steam-driven machinery is better seen as a symbol of, rather than the cause of, rapid economic growth in the West. Without the underlying changes that supported industrial growth, peripheral nations could import the latest machinery only to watch it fall into disrepair, as happened in Egypt under Muhammad Ali.

We can accept the complex origins of the Industrial Revolution in Europe, however, without throwing out the idea that industrialization changed the world radically. Think of it this way. Steam-powered factories only become common after 1800; the earliest railroads date from the 1830s; electricity and telephones came into use after 1880; automobiles and airplanes date from the early 1900s. That timeline means that, in less than 200 years, factories, trains, electricity, cars, and air travel have fundamentally reshaped human society. If you open any newspaper to the obituaries, you will find lucky souls who lived well into their 90s. Put two such long lives together and you have over 180 years—meaning that the industrial age has remade the world in the equivalent of two lifetimes, though admittedly long ones. That *is* revolutionary.

People who lived through these changes saw them as revolutionary. A Scottish merchant, Patrick Coquhoun, wrote in 1814 that "it is impossible to contemplate the progress of manufactures in Great Britain within the last thirty years without wonder and astonishment."[5] Poets William Blake and William Wordsworth lamented the rapid changes in British society caused by industrial growth, while

Charles Dickens recorded the human cost of industrialization in many of his novels. In *Hard Times* (1854), Dickens describes one of the new industrial cities that had grown up in England's green midlands.

> It was a town of red brick, or of brick that would have been red if the smoke and ashes had allowed it . . . It was a town of machinery and tall chimneys, out of which interminable serpents of smoke trailed . . . It had a black canal in it, and a river that ran purple with ill-smelling dye. . . . It contained several large streets all very like one another, and many small streets still more like one another, inhabited by people equally like one another, who all went in and out at the same hours, with the same sound upon the same pavements, to do the same work, and to whom every day was the same as yesterday and to-morrow, and every year the counterpart of the last and the next.[6]

The men, women, and children who worked in factories like the ones Dickens describes did not enjoy better lives than their grandparents, who had farmed the land. Yet, by doing "the same work . . . every day . . . and every year," they made Britain the world's leading industrial power.

In the countries and regions where it took hold, the Industrial Revolution turned artisans into factory laborers, farm women into domestic servants. But the spread of factories also changed the nature of ruling elites. Aristocrats—princes, dukes, lords, and so on—had dominated Europe because land, which they monopolized, was the premodern world's main source of wealth. The new industries allowed a new class to accumulate huge amounts of wealth, dwarfing even the riches of kings and queens. Karl Marx called this new class the *bourgeoisie* and the new economic system *capitalism.*

THE INDUSTRIAL REVOLUTION AND WESTERN POWER

Industry made England rich and powerful. As the English intellectual Robert Owen noted in 1815, the immediate effect of the Industrial Revolution was "a rapid increase in the wealth, industry, population and political influence of the British Empire."[7] For government leaders, the new wealth and technology meant one thing above all—military power. Industrialized nations poured money into new weapons—steam-driven, steel-hulled battleships, long-range cannon, machine guns, and rifles being the most important in the 19th century.

As the world's first industrial nation, Britain dominated the 19th-century world. British leaders used the country's newfound wealth to build the world's greatest navy and through the 19th century built an empire that girded the globe—hence the old saying that "the sun never sets on the British Empire." William Gladstone, Britain's prime minister, boasted in 1879 that for the first time in history "a small island at one extremity of the globe peoples the whole earth with its colonies."[8]

If Europeans had little doubt about the revolutionary impact of industrialization, rulers outside Europe could hardly ignore the dramatic increase in Western power. Nations and empires that had beat back or simply ignored Western power before 1800—Japan, China, India, the Ottoman Empire—now had to come to terms with it. China had had direct contact with the West since ancient times, but managed to keep the "barbarians" at arm's length, officially banning Europeans in the 1630s. The Ottoman Turks, whose territory extended into southeastern Europe, had for centuries been powerful enough not only to defend themselves against European armies but to launch incursions into Europe's heartland.

After 1800, the relative power of these two vast states declined radically. It is no coincidence that both the Ottomans and China succumbed to British power in the same decade, when that small island nation had advanced its precocious Industrial Revolution for half a century. In the 1830s, the Chinese government ordered British merchants to stop selling opium, a narcotic that they were importing from India. In the Opium Wars of 1838–1841, Britain's modern navy easily defeated the war junks of the Celestial Empire, as China called itself. The Ottomans, intimidated by British naval power, caved in to Britain's demands for "economic capitulations" in 1838. If these great empires could not resist the newly forged power of the West, how could smaller and less-organized societies in Asia, Africa, the Middle East, or Latin America hope to do so?

Although British economists like Adam Smith and David Ricardo praised free trade among nations, British officials did not shy away from using naval power to open doors to her exports. Having defeated the Chinese and intimidated the Ottomans, Britain imposed on both empires commercial treaties that lowered tariffs on British products. The effects were felt immediately. "Manufacturing industry has greatly declined from what it formerly was in the Ottoman Empire," a visitor to Istanbul noted in 1856. "At present the greater part of the exports of Turkey consist of raw materials which it hands over to Europe, and which the latter returns to Turkey in a manufactured form. The numerous and varied manufactures . . . no longer exist or have completely declined."[9]

Like the use of force to impose unequal treaties, the growth of Britain's empire also contradicted the principle of free trade. Most of the Indian subcontinent came under direct British rule after 1857, meaning that London henceforth set India's economic policies. Not surprisingly, British officials set Indian tariffs so low that British goods flowed into the colony. Indian economic historian Romesh Dutt noted in 1904 that "the commercial policy of the British rulers of India has been determined, not by the interests of Indian manufacturers, but by those of British manufacturers."[10] Indian exports of cotton clothing plunged due to "the rapid substitution of British cotton goods in the international market for India's export products followed by a rising flood of imports into India itself."[11] Britain boasted that it had become the workshop of the world, but by doing so it had *de*industrialized areas that had once exported handmade goods. Indeed, before the advent of modern industry in the West, artisans in the future periphery, Asia in particular, produced something like 75 percent of the world's manufactured goods. By 1900 the world economy had a new structure, with a core of industrial nations drawing raw materials, such as cotton, minerals, and foods, from the periphery and selling back finished goods made in modern factories.

SHOCK AND AWE IN THE PERIPHERY

The West's challenge to premodern societies went beyond manufacturing and military science. Not only did non-European peoples confront Western navies and machine-made goods, but also Western diplomatic protocols and standards of hygiene, Western definitions of private property, Western modes of dress, Western styles of journalism and literature—in a word, an entire way of life and state of mind. The West's challenge must have seemed astonishingly complete to peoples outside Europe and the United States. The violent encounter of traditional and modern societies is brilliantly imagined by Nigerian writer Chinua Achebe in the novel *Things Fall Apart*, which shows how British missionaries and officials turned local culture on its head, making the former outcasts of one Igbo village into powerful agents of the new foreign rulers.

Faced by the overwhelming material power of the West, many intellectuals in Asia, Africa, and Latin America turned against the traditions and customs of their homelands. "I unreservedly condemn our Eastern civilization and warmly praise the modern civilization of the West," wrote Hu Shi, a young Chinese intellectual who studied at Columbia University in the first years of the 20th century.[12] Modernizers like Hu Shi fervently believed that their societies had to change radically to succeed in a world dominated by the West. To them, there was no question that the West had made itself into something fundamentally different from—and at least in material terms, clearly superior to—the premodern societies they inhabited. The Industrial Revolution, historian Michael Adas writes, "steadily widened the gap in material productivity and mastery of the natural world between Western Europeans and the rest of humanity."[13] To modernizers the problem could be stated baldly: What must we do to close the gap with the West? Most wanted to conserve their own culture while adopting enough of the West's modernity to defend themselves from foreign control. Japanese reformers called this hybrid of modernity and tradition *Wakon Yosai*, which means "Western learning, Japanese spirit."

By 1850, then, a few nations had become identifiably "modern." In this handful of countries, industry grew, transportation accelerated,

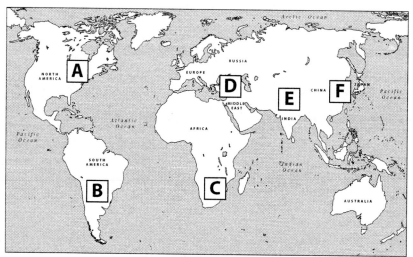

MAP I.1 World Industrial Zones. This world map and the details on the next page show how modern manufacturing had spread globally by about 1900.

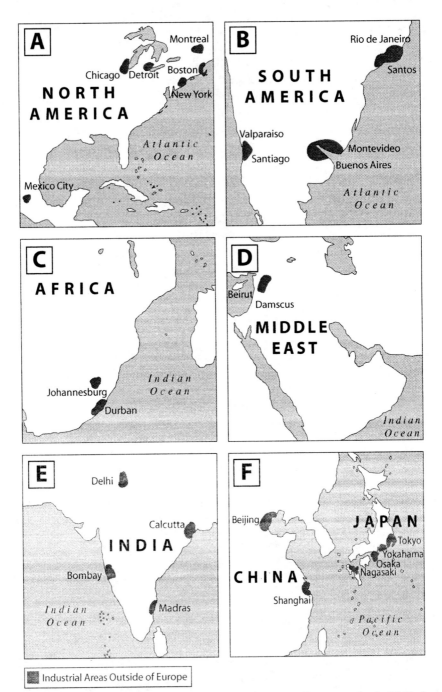

MAP I.2 Outside the industrial heartland of Western Europe, only the United States and Japan (shown in details A and F) had become major industrial powers. In the rest of Asia and in Africa, Latin America and the Middle East, industrialization remained very limited.

literacy increased, life expectancy improved, and political participation expanded. Yet most of the world remained nonindustrial, and
for the most part lifestyles in those countries and colonies were what
we have been calling *premodern*. To understand the magnitude of the
challenge faced by modernizers in Asia, Africa, and Latin America, let
us sketch some broad differences between premodern and modern
societies.

THE PREMODERN WORLD

Although there was great diversity among preindustrial peoples, all
premodern societies—meaning the entire world before the 1800s—
shared certain basic characteristics. The single most important was
scarcity—of almost everything. Food was often scarce, even though
most people were farmers, because productivity was low at best and
often dipped lower due to droughts, plagues, floods, and wars. Population density was also much lower than in the industrial age.
Premodern societies were essentially rural, with some small towns
and very few cities. In 1790, after 150 years of growth, the preindustrial cities of Boston and New York had 28,000 and 33,000 people,
respectively—the size of small towns today. There were some large
premodern cities: Hangzhou, in China, had over a million people by
1200 CE, while the Aztec capital at Tenochtitlan (where Mexico City
now stands) astonished Hernán Cortés with its huge buildings and a
population greater than that of Seville. Still, the generalization
holds—premodern life was rural, not urban. As mechanized agriculture spread across the planet, population increased rapidly. The
world's population had barely reached 1 billion by 1800. Today, only
200 years after the Industrial Revolution began, the planet supports
more than 6 billion people.

Another fact of premodern life was scarcity of material goods.
All products—wagons, tools, furniture, clothing—had to be made
painstakingly by hand. By modern standards, a typical premodern
home was small and practically empty—a few tools, some metal pots,
one set of clothes for cold, another for warm weather. If you have read
Little House in the Big Woods, you are familiar with one premodern society. In that memoir, Laura Ingalls Wilder describes her childhood on
the Minnesota frontier in the 1880s. Living far from the factories of the
Midwest, her family made nearly everything they needed in their own

home—spinning wool to make clothing, slaughtering pigs and preserving the meat, putting up fruit and vegetables, and even melting lead to cast bullets for the family rifle. Like the Ingalls family, preindustrial people elsewhere consumed very little by our standards—in fact, the whole concept of *consumers* (as opposed to *producers*) is a very modern one. For one thing, there wasn't much to buy, and they had little money to spend. Indeed, in many parts of the premodern world people never handled money at all but instead bartered what they produced for what they needed.

Of course, there *was* trade and commerce long before the Industrial Revolution. Shopkeepers sold goods in towns across China, Africa, Europe, and South America, and market fairs brought farmers and artisans from miles around. Even so, before canals, railroads, and highways lowered transportation costs, trade was restricted and few merchants got rich. For the same reason, there was little savings or accumulated capital to be invested in new ventures. Kings, queens, and emperors lived in luxury, as a glance at the castles of Europe confirms, as did some very wealthy merchants and bankers in Venice, Florence, and other European cities. Still, wealth in private hands was relatively limited until the Industrial Revolution radically increased productivity and thus allowed the accumulation of vast private fortunes—think of John D. Rockefeller in the petroleum business, Henry Ford and the automobile, and Andrew Carnegie's steel empire, for example.

Another type of premodern scarcity was more abstract. We might call this the scarcity of national identity. Premodern societies were overwhelmingly rural, and farmers rarely traveled far from home. Living in the countryside, their strongest loyalties were local—*my* town, *my* village. Each region usually had its own special foods and typical clothing, its own history and folklore, even its own dialect and gods (or saints). To pull these many scattered farms and tiny villages together and give them a sense of national identity was no easy task even in Europe, where "nationalism" first took root. In the early 1800s, for example, German-speaking people were spread across dozens of kingdoms, city-states, and duchies in Western Europe and had no sense of themselves as a nation. One reason the Grimm brothers set out to collect stories like "Cinderella," "Snow White," and others told by German-speaking peasants was to make them conscious that they all belonged to a single German "fatherland."[14]

The point is that *nationalism*—pride in one's homeland, the willingness to take up arms to defend the national flag—is a modern phenomenon that had to be constructed. In Europe, the Industrial Revolution helped build nations out of scattered communities. Roads and then railroads knit together far-flung regions. Towns and cities grew into centers of trade and industry, drawing migrants from the countryside. As peasants moved to the city, they took on new identities. Many went to school for the first time and there learned to read—and public schools everywhere became cradles of nationalism. "Every powerful nation in Europe," a Japanese advocate of mandatory schooling told his countrymen in 1890, "strives to foster through public education a deep sense of patriotism."[15] Books and newspapers were written in national languages, not local dialects. French and German schoolchildren, for example, drank in the idea that they were part of a single culture in a larger world. Love of *la patrie* or *das Vaterland* became as natural to them as the need for sunlight and air.

Nationalism changed the face of Europe. Italy came together slowly as a single nation by the 1860s, while a unified Germany did not emerge until 1871. The process continued in the 20th century, often helped along by world wars that shattered empires like Austria-Hungary. When old empires broke apart, their fragments came together as new nations.

As Western Europe industrialized and urbanized, the nature of government changed as well. In premodern times, ordinary people had little to say about how they were ruled. To peasant farmers, political events in far-off capitals mattered little as long as harvests were good. The kings, queens, and princes who ruled the premodern world often had little in common with their subjects. England's King George I was a German speaker from Hanover who never bothered to learn the language of Shakespeare. The rulers of the Ottoman Empire spoke Turkish; the majority of their subjects did not. But as the urban, literate, laboring population grew, kings and queens could no longer safely ignore what we now call "public opinion"—another modern concept. The new urban classes—shopkeepers and factory workers, clerks and servants—read newspapers and voiced their opinions when governments hiked taxes and started wars. So it was that industrialization and nationalism encouraged the growth of democracy. By 1900, most men could vote in Western Europe and the United States—although in the latter case only white men actually exercised the franchise.

FROM PREMODERN TO MODERN

Premodern societies were not as static and incapable of change as the snapshot above suggests, as will become clear when we look at Japan. By making a binary division of the world into modern and premodern, we are flirting with an oversimplification that many historians would reject. The goal is not to reproduce the arrogance of earlier generations by assuming, as Michael Adas warns, that "modernity is associated with rationality, empiricism, efficiency and progressive change," while "tradition connotes fatalism, veneration for custom and the sacred, indiscipline, and stagnation."[16] Let us be clear, then, that this division is not absolute and that the societies we are calling premodern or traditional were highly varied and undergoing change at their own pace. Beneath the myriad local variations, however, the basic outlines of the premodern world persisted for thousands of years.

Before industrialization, the gap between Western Europe and the rest of the world was relatively minor. One African historian notes that "pre-colonial Africa had a range of manufacturing industries which closely resembled that of pre-industrial societies in other parts of the world . . . based on clothing, metal working, ceramics, construction, and food processing."[17] Economic historian Paul Bairoch argues that "there was a parity of income per capita for the average future Third World and developed countries before the latter region started to undergo the process of modern economic growth."[18] The Industrial Revolution ended the *parity*, or equality, that Bairoch notes. By 1910 the average income in England was six times more, and by 1950 ten times more, than the average in China.[19]

It is worth mentioning that the leap to modernity was not painless even in nations that made the transition early. The first nations to industrialize—Britain, Germany, and the United States—themselves had to overcome considerable resistance to change. Farmers and artisans were not eager to give up their independence and become factory workers. Once economic pressure forced men, women, and children into factories, they resisted the life-killing routine of 12-hour days, 6 days a week. It took decades for industrial, urban life to become "normal" even in the most advanced societies. By the time it did, the industrial nations had far outstripped less-developed countries.

And, despite the harsh conditions faced by factory workers, overall conditions improved rapidly in the industrial West. In Europe and the United States, cities provided clean drinking water and built sewer systems, reducing outbreaks of cholera and other infectious diseases. Fewer people died of disease, and more lived to be senior citizens. They also grew taller—several inches taller—than their grandparents and than people in less-developed countries. As late as 1950, people in developed countries could expect to live into their late sixties, while those in less-developed countries barely reached 40 (on average).[20] In developed countries, most adults learned to read and write, while in the periphery 80 percent or more of adults were illiterate.

Women's lives also changed radically. In earlier times, peasant women married young and often had ten or more pregnancies. They spent much of their adult lives pregnant or caring for infants, and many died in childbirth. As countries industrialized, families increasingly practiced birth control, so average family size dropped even though fewer children died in their first years.

European and American visitors to less-developed countries and colonies found old-fashioned work habits amusing, as the captions for this Western postcard from China and the one from Korea on the next page suggest.

As was true in Europe before the Industrial Revolution, human labor, not machinery, got the job done in premodern societies.

COMING TO GRIPS WITH THE WEST

The gap between modern and premodern nations was never greater than at the turn of the 19th century. Traditional lifestyles, which had persisted for thousands of years, now seemed primitive and barbaric to "modern" people. An English visitor traveling through a remote but inhabited region of the Middle East in 1890 was astonished by what he called the "great withoutness" of the premodern world. It was "a country without roads. . . . without shops. . . . without regular posts [mail service]. . . . without newspapers. . . . without schools . . . without doctors and hospitals."[21] European and American visitors to the periphery often commented on the way premodern people worked. The postcards from China and Korea show how traditional ways of cutting and hauling wood amused Westerners who had only recently become accustomed to power saws and railroads and further suggest the condescension of Western visitors to the nonindustrial peoples of the world.

CATCHING THE WEST: PRECOCIOUS EGYPT

Meanwhile, the premodern societies that received European and American visitors reached their own conclusions about what modernity was. At first, they naturally focused on the inventions that were the most visible sign of the Industrial Revolution—gunboats, steam engines, railroads, and so on. People living far from the industrial centers of Europe and the United States—in China and Japan, Egypt and Ethiopia, Mexico and Argentina, even Russia and Turkey—initially made the error of seeing Western power in strictly technological terms. If industry gave the West the huge material advantage it had so recently gained on the rest of the world, why not cut short the long process of development and leap into modernity, importing the new technologies, hiring the best European engineers, and forcing peasants off the land to work in brand-new factories? In other words, why not use government power to accelerate the transition to modernity?

The first "latecomer" to launch a crash program to catch up with the West was Egypt, and the leader of this precocious modernization movement was Muhammad Ali (1769?–1849). Muhammad Ali was an official of the Ottoman Empire who had been born in Macedonia, in Ottoman Europe. In 1805 he became the *pasha*, or governor, of Egypt, at the time still part of the Ottoman Empire. The new ruler had been powerfully impressed by the efficiency of the French army when Napoleon Bonaparte had invaded Egypt in 1798. Illiterate himself, Muhammad Ali nevertheless understood that industry was transforming Britain and France into a new kind of world power. Beginning in 1815, he tried to force-march Egypt toward modernity—the first of many rulers to try to use the power of the state to achieve a "great leap forward."

The pasha of Egypt first set out to transform agriculture. Cotton, the raw material that fed England's booming textile mills, grew in Egypt, not Europe. Why not grow more cotton and weave it into cloth in Egypt? To that end, Muhammad Ali did away with the ancient practice of communal landholding, had new irrigation channels built, and introduced the planting of high-quality, long-fiber cotton. As cotton production boomed, he imported power looms and technicians from Europe. Soon Egypt had factories that turned out not only cotton, wool, and other textiles but also paper, glass, sugar, and chemicals. Because Muhammad Ali's goal was to make Egypt modern and powerful, he also built an arsenal "where the skilled workmen of England and Europe directed the industry of hundreds of native Egyptians in the casting of cannon," as an early observer noted.[22] Trained by European officers in Egypt's new military schools, his well-equipped army outmatched the troops of the sultan in Istanbul, to whom Muhammad Ali supposedly owed complete loyalty.

By the early 1830s, it appeared that Muhammad Ali had succeeded in bringing the Industrial Revolution to North Africa, well before industry had spread through most of Europe. Below the surface, however, there were grave problems. Muhammad Ali cared about the power and wealth of Egypt more than he did about the well-being of Egyptians. To raise money, the pasha imposed new taxes on peasants, the vast majority of Egypt's population. He made the cotton trade a state monopoly, buying cotton at a low fixed price from poor farmers, selling it at high price to Europeans, and using the profit to finance his modernizing drive. For labor to build the canals and irrigation ditches that Egypt needed, the pasha commanded peasants to leave their fields and work under a system of *corveé*, or compulsory labor. To expand his army, Muhammad Ali sent officials to scour villages and draft young men by force if need be. In many villages, men cut off fingers and toes to escape military service. The pasha's attempt to transform Egypt overnight came at a high price for ordinary Egyptians.

Muhammad Ali's "great leap forward" in Egypt attracted much attention in Europe. Visitors marveled at the new factories, canals, schools, hospitals, and army that Muhammad Ali had built. Edward William Lane, an Englishman who visited in the mid-1820s, praised Egypt's progress even as he criticized the pasha's harsh rule. The pasha "devoted large sums of money to the establishment of fabrics [factories] for the weaving of woolen, cotton, and linen cloths, and of silks," Lane wrote, ". . . but the nation has suffered very severely from his monopoly of those manufactures." Lane noted that Egyptian peasants bore the burden of their ruler's ambitious program. Muhammad Ali had indeed increased the output of farms "by digging new canals, . . . thus fertilizing large tracts of land . . . but he has impoverished the inhabitants—I might almost say that he has ruined and famished them—by monopolizing the produce of the fields, and all the principal manufactures. . . . He has reduced the whole of the Egyptian peasantry almost to the condition of slaves."[23]

As we shall see, Muhammad Ali was the first, but not the last, modernizer to subject his people to the hardships of state-sponsored industrialization. Unlike the industrial transformation of England, pushed forward by the activity of thousands of private manufacturers, inventors, and investors, modernization in Egypt came from the top down, by order of the pasha. Every new project—canals, factories, plantations, hospitals, schools—was imposed by the government. In short, the drive to remake Egypt put Muhammad Ali in conflict with his own people.

By the time Muhammad Ali died in 1849, his dream of a modern, industrialized Egypt was falling apart. The sultan of the Ottoman Empire had watched anxiously as Muhammad Ali, technically his vassal, transformed Egypt and built a powerful army. Britain, too, worried about Egypt's growing power. When Muhammad Ali sent his army against the sultan, Britain took the side of the Ottoman ruler against the Egyptian upstart. Defeated, Muhammad Ali agreed to reduce the size of his army. In his last years, the pasha watched many of his pet projects collapse.

CATCHING THE WEST: MEIJI JAPAN

Egypt's drive to modernize presents a striking contrast to that of Japan some 50 years later. Japan in the 1800s had long excluded Westerners from its shores, with the exception of a single Dutch ship that was allowed to dock each year at an offshore landfill in Nagasaki harbor. After Britain forced China to open itself to wider trade in the 1840s, the United States sent an expedition under Commodore Matthew Perry to "encourage" Japan to end its virtual isolation from the West. Perry sailed into the harbor at Edo (present-day Tokyo) in 1853, making clear to the Japanese emperor that if his "pacific overtures" were ignored, he would take stronger measures against the hermit kingdom. By 1858, Japan had signed treaties that not only allowed trade with the West, but also limited the tariffs that Japan could impose on imports. The treaties further humiliated Japan by granting *extraterritoriality*, meaning, as one sailor put it, that "Americans shall . . . be subject solely to American law" as applied by U.S. consuls in Japan. Extraterritoriality assumed that the Japanese had not reached a level of civilization adequate to pass judgment on foreigners.[24]

Thus far, Japan seemed to be following China, India, and the Ottoman Empire toward economic domination by the West. Yet, remarkably, Japan's future was very different. Faced with the clear threat of foreign control, a group of reformers—mostly military men known as *samurai*—seized power in the name of Emperor Meiji. Over the next decades, these leaders orchestrated the transformation of Japan, largely succeeding where Muhammad Ali had failed 50 years earlier.

The new rulers of Japan moved swiftly to secure their political control by reducing the power of local leaders, called *daimyo*, who until then had their own armies and sources of revenue. The reformers then ordered a survey of every parcel of land in the nation, the basis of a new tax on property. On this solid structure, the reformers then launched the most extraordinary example of planned cultural borrowing the world has seen. The Meiji rulers understood that catching up with the West involved much more than buying foreign gunboats and importing naval experts to train Japanese crews. The country had to transform itself economically and politically to become a power able to compete with Europe and the United States. Meiji officials boiled the challenge down to the pithy phrase *Fukoku Kyohei*, meaning "rich country, strong army."

In the early 1870s, the Meiji reformers sent out "missions" to study the many areas in which the West was more advanced. Missions visited the United States and Europe, where they studied shipyards and factories, colleges and high schools, military academies and railroad terminals, statehouses and churches. The West took notice of Japan's ambitious modernization program. American newspapers reported regularly on the arrival of Japanese students and officials. The Iwakura Mission, a group of over 50 officials who arrived in California in the winter of 1871 and toured the United States for seven months, was followed everywhere by curious reporters. "Japanese Scouring the World after Knowledge," the *New York Times* reported, noting that the Japanese seemed intelligent and well-informed, even though they came from a "heathen" and "semi-civilized" nation.

Based on the detailed observations of the missions, as well as the knowledge that Japanese students gained abroad and the help of thousands of *o-yatoi*, or foreign advisors, who trained Japanese in key areas, the Meiji reformers moved quickly. Understanding the link between knowledge and power, in 1872 they began to build a modern public school system. By 1880, 40 percent of school-age children were attending classes; by 1900, the number had jumped to 90 percent. The government also built universities, technical schools, and agricultural colleges. Industrial growth was a priority, but first Japan needed infrastructure. In 1871, the country began delivering mail for the first time; within three years 3,000 post offices dotted the national territory. The government hired foreign engineers to build the first rail lines to connect inland cities to seaports and then link Tokyo to Osaka and Kyoto. To provide money for the projects, the reformers encouraged an increase in traditional export products such as silk, tea, and ceramics. Silk exports doubled in 15 years. The government also opened a central bank to promote investment.

As it had in Egypt under Muhammad Ali, modernization in Japan involved a vast increase in the government's power over everyday life. Besides encouraging industry and education, the government tried to persuade citizens to wear Western clothing, eat bread instead of rice, and consume more meat, as Westerners did. Not all reforms got a warm reception from the Japanese people.

Efforts to launch modern industry faltered at first. The reformers did not want foreigners to build up Japan's manufacturing base, but local capital was scarce. The government decided it had to champion the factory system itself and built steam-powered cement, glass, and brick factories as well as modern ironworks, shipyards, and munitions plants. In Japan as in Egypt, workers at first had trouble handling the new machinery. One Meiji official noted that even if Japanese "order machinery from abroad, they cannot operate it."[25] They learned, however, and soon Japanese supervisors replaced foreigners even in highly skilled jobs. By the 1880s the government was able to sell the model factories to Japanese owners. This success encouraged private investors to move into new areas, especially cotton and silk textile production. Industrial transformation became self-sustaining.

Japan modernized rapidly from the 1870s to the 1890s, and as it did the country's attitude toward the West also evolved. In the early years, Japanese leaders were overawed by the West. "If we compare the knowledge of the Japanese and Westerners," Fukuzawa Yukichi, a leading intellectual, wrote in the 1870s, ". . . . there is not one thing in which we excel. . . . Who would compare our carts with their locomotives, or our swords with their pistols? . . . . All that Japan has to be proud of . . . is its scenery."[26] By the 1880s, Japan had moved beyond admiring all things Western. In 1889, the journalist Kuga Katsunan could write that "we respect Western philosophy and morals . . . Above all, we esteem Western science, economics and industry. These, however, ought not to be adopted simply because they are Western; they ought to be adopted only if they can contribute to Japan's welfare."[27]

The real test of Japan's "civilization" turned out to be war. In 1894, Japan fought China, its ancient role model, and decisively defeated the Celestial Empire. "We are no longer ashamed to stand before the world as Japanese," one well-known journalist wrote after that victory.[28] The West saw with surprise that Japan now treated China as a semi-barbarous nation, just as the West had treated Japan. Japan applied another lesson learned from the West, using its military victory to gain privileged access to Chinese markets. American newspapers frankly admired the "plucky little island empire," and Japan at last negotiated an end to the unequal treaties imposed after Perry's visit. For the first time, a nation in the periphery had earned the respect of the West on the battlefield. The message seemed clear: In the eyes of the West, military power was the measure of civilization.

Why did Japan succeed where Egypt had failed? Much had to do with the conditions that existed before Commodore Perry arrived in Japan. Although isolated from the West, Japan had a thriving internal economy by the 1700s. Tokyo had a population of 1 million in 1700, making it the largest city in the world; Osaka and Kyoto were the size of London and Paris at the time. Good roads connected the cities and the countryside, where farmers raised crops for urban markets, rather than for mere subsistence. Proto-industry also thrived in Japan's countryside, with farm families raising silk and producing lacquer ware and other ceramics. In short, before the West "opened" Japan, that nation was already moving beyond the premodern conditions described earlier in this chapter, becoming an urban, commercial society. When the opening came, Japanese merchants, artisans, and farmers were able to adapt quickly, if not painlessly, to the change.

THE PERIPHERY FIGHTS BACK

Egypt from 1815 to the 1840s and Japan from 1868 to 1895 offer contrasting examples of *defensive modernization*. Although Egypt advanced under Muhammad Ali, it did not achieve the self-sustaining growth that Japan had by the 1890s. Japan's achievement was astonishing, and unique: No other peripheral nation succeeded in modernizing as thoroughly before World War I. Japan's transformation, however, is not an entirely happy story. The Meiji reformers were more excited by material progress than by democracy, which they kept carefully controlled. They also used military spending as a permanent stimulus to Japan's heavy industries, building a powerful army and navy. Proof of their strategy's success came again in 1904–1905, when Japan went to war with, and soundly trounced, Russia. Russia's defeat at the hands of an Asian power humiliated the tsar and nearly led to his overthrow a dozen years before the Bolshevik Revolution. The Japanese, meanwhile, saw themselves as the "natural" leaders of Asia and began to build an empire, starting with Taiwan and Korea. Their push to replace Western imperialism in Asia with their own *hegemony*, or domination, led to the invasion of China in 1937 and the attack on Pearl Harbor in 1941.

By the late 1800s, nationalist leaders in the periphery realized that catching up with the West did not simply mean importing machinery and hiring European generals to train their armies. They understood that their societies had to change profoundly, from top to bottom, in order to harness the energy and skills of the entire population. "I am keenly aware that the wealth and power of the European nations are the result not only of their having ships and powerful guns," wrote the young Sun Yatsen, future leader of China, ". . . but also because their people can fully employ their talents, their land can be fully utilized, their natural resources can be fully tapped, and their goods can freely flow."[29]

By the early 20th century, the cult of modernization in the developing world was so much a fact of life that it was even parodied by witty writers in the West. British novelist Evelyn Waugh, a merciless critic of his own society, offered a scathing portrait of the Emperor Seth, the European-educated ruler of a made-up African kingdom in his 1932 novel *Black Mischief*. Battling to hold on to power against the rebel leader Seyid, Seth proclaims,

> I am Seth, grandson of Amurath. Defeat is impossible. I have been to Europe. I know. We have the Tank. This is not a war of Seth against Seyid but of Progress against Barbarism. And Progress must prevail. I have seen . . . the Paris Exhibition, the Oxford Union. I have read modern books—Shaw, Arlen, Priestley. What do the gossips in the bazaars know of all this? . . . At my stirrups run woman's suffrage, vaccination, and vivisection. I am the New Age. I am the Future.[30]

MODERNIZATION IN THE COLONIES

The focus of this book is defensive modernization in four independent nations in the periphery. From the late 1800s through World War II, however, much of the nonindustrial world was not independent but rather under European control. It is worth looking briefly at how the colonies experienced "modernity." Colonial authorities did not wish to turn their premodern possessions into industrial competitors, but they did want colonial subjects to produce goods for export rather than "languishing" as subsistence farmers, herders, and nomads. Left to their own devices, the Europeans noted, tropical peoples would never embrace progress. They had to be forced into the future.

In the African colonies of Britain, France, Belgium, and Portugal, officials resorted to forced labor to construct the infrastructure needed for export-based economies. "European productive enterprises," a member of the Belgian Colonial Council explained in 1928, "cannot be carried out, at the present moment, without obligatory labour."[31] Even "liberal" Britain resorted to compulsion to build railroads in East Africa since "where there are railways to-day there is development." That logic justified a policy making it "compulsory for the natives to work on railways in which they are so directly interested." Economic development was, after all, part of the *mission civilisatrice* that justified

In European colonies in Africa and Asia, officials forced local people to build the transportation systems needed to create an export-based economy. In the Belgian Congo, Africans lay the rails that would carry ivory, rubber and other products to the world market.

European rule over nearly all of Africa. "We have a duty to humanity to develop the vast economic resources of a great continent," British officials declared, and they had no compunction about requiring Africans to participate in that project whether they wished to or not.[32]

Given such policies, it is not surprising that colonial subjects across Africa and Asia organized against foreign rule. More unexpected is the fact that nationalist leaders often advocated the same model of development as colonial officials. For example, an elite of Indians educated in British schools began to push for greater "home rule" by the late 1800s. These early nationalists did not call for independence from Britain. Instead, they wanted educated Indians—that is, themselves—to have a larger voice in government even as India remained a British colony. In fact, this Indian elite gave thanks to the empire for bringing India "the advantages of good roads, railways, telegraphs and post-offices, schools, colleges and universities, hospitals, good laws and impartial courts of justice."[33] One Indian historian goes so far as to note that for the nationalist elites "the main enemy was not British rule as such, but the backwardness of the people." They did not want the "ignorant peasants" who made up the vast majority of India's population to vote. Instead, they hoped that education and economic development would, over many years, prepare India's hundreds of millions of peasants for self-government. "There can be no doubt that the permanent salvation of the Country depends upon the growth of Indian Manufactures and Commerce," Indian reform leader Mahadev Govind Ranade declared in 1899.[34] In other words, the early nationalists, much like British officials themselves, saw economic modernization as a necessary first step before independence and self-rule.

THE STRUCTURE OF THIS BOOK

The rest of this book will focus on modernizing drives in four very different countries—Mexico, Ethiopia, China, and Turkey. These four case studies encompass diverse regions—from Latin America to the Middle East, East Africa to East Asia. They also cover nearly three-quarters of a century, beginning in the 1870s in Mexico and concluding in the 1930s with Turkey. This broad sweep of space and time is made more manageable by a sharp focus on the modernization strategies of four strong leaders—Porfirio Díaz in Mexico (lived 1830–1915, in power 1877–1911), Menelik II in Ethiopia (lived 1844–1913, in power

1889–1909), Sun Yatsen in China (lived 1866–1925, in power only briefly but influential from 1905 until his death), and Mustafa Kemal in Turkey (lived 1881–1938, in power from 1923 until his death).

Because defensive modernization was a primary goal of many independent nations after 1830, we might have examined other cases. We could, for example, have included King Mongkut (lived 1804–1868, in power 1851–1868) of Thailand, whose story is captured in the play and film *The King and I.* Mongkut promoted education and economic development even as he played a clever diplomatic game to balance British and French power and thus preserve his nation's independence. In Latin America, we could easily have selected Domingo Sarmiento (lived 1811–1888, in power 1868–1874), a leading Argentinean intellectual who as president led his country toward economic modernity at the expense of genuine democracy. Many others could be added to this list of defensive modernizers.

The four cases we look at here thus reflect a larger trend that encompassed the entire globe and defined much of world history after 1800. Unlike the cases of Egypt and Japan outlined above, the four cases we will explore in this book are neither clear-cut success stories nor abysmal failures. Their ambiguity makes them more representative of experiences in other less-developed countries—Brazil and Argentina, Iran and India, Vietnam and the Philippines, among many others— where modernization partially transformed older ways of life but has not achieved material well-being for a majority of the people. Every country is unique, every history is distinct, yet the four cases that follow explore defensive modernization as a dynamic that shaped much of the nonindustrial world from the mid-1800s through the 20th century.

As the cases of Egypt and Japan demonstrate, nationalist leaders in the periphery understood the weakness of their societies relative to the West and applied harsh policies to push their nations toward modernity. Still, three of the leaders examined here—all but Porfirio Díaz—are still considered "founding fathers" of their nations. That is indeed ironic, since all four leaders had more in common, in terms of their ambitions and visions of the future, with Americans or Europeans than they did with the peasant majorities in their homelands. As nationalists, these leaders were willing to sacrifice everything for their nations. As disciples of the West, however, they demanded that their people change radically. They were nationalist leaders who were in many ways profoundly *de*nationalized.

For all their differences, the four nationalist leaders that you will read about in the coming chapters had much in common. All accepted that Europe and the United States had developed a new kind of progress that had to be imported into their countries. All struggled to find a workable balance of tradition and modernity, and each tried to import capital and technology without giving up national sovereignty. All believed that state power had to be deployed, often ruthlessly, to catch up with the West. All accepted the use of violence not only to prevent foreign control of their homelands, but also to transform their societies in the face of resistance by their own people.

This book's final chapter, Making Connections, looks ahead to a new paradigm for modernization that emerged after World War I—Communism. Starting in the early 1920s the newly founded Soviet Union vigorously promoted a socialist command economy as the true road to development in the periphery, lumping capitalism and imperialism together as the enemies of nonindustrial countries and colonies. In the aftermath of World War II, as colonialism ended and dozens of new nations emerged, the competition between the capitalist and Communist paths to modernity became the crux of the Cold War and the defining issue of the late 20th century. Although the Cold War is over, the struggle to achieve modernity is not—the promise of modernization and the obstacles to achieving it remain burning issues across Asia, Africa, the Middle East, Latin America, and the Caribbean.

NOTES

1. William McNeill, *The Rise of the West* (Chicago: University of Chicago, 1963).
2. Sheldon Garon, "Rethinking Modernization and Modernity in Japanese History: A Focus on State-Society Relations," *Journal of Asian Studies* 53: 2 (May 1994), p. 347.
3. Tetsuo Najita, "Presidential Address: Reflections on Modernity and Modernization," *Journal of Asian Studies* 52: 4 (November 1993), p. 850.
4. N.F.R. Crafts, "Industrial Revolution in England and France: Some Thoughts on the Question, 'Why was England First?' " *Economic History Review* 30: 3 (August 1977), p. 430.
5. Quoted in Joel Mokyr, Introduction, *The British Industrial Revolution* (Boulder: Westview, 1993), p. 3.
6. Charles Dickens, *Hard Times* (London: Oxford University Press, 1955), p. 22.
7. Quoted in Mokyr, *British Industrial Revolution*, p. 3.
8. Joseph Hendershot Park, *British Prime Ministers of the Nineteenth Century* (Freeport, NY: Books for Libraries Press, 1970), pp. 283–284.
9. Quoted in Kemal H. Karpat, "The Transformation of the Ottoman State, 1789–1908," *International Journal of Middle East Studies* 3: 3 (July 1972), p. 247.
10. Romesh Chunder Dutt, *India in the Victorian Age: An Economic History of the People* (Delhi: Daya Publishing, 1985), p. vii.

11. K.N. Chaudhuri, "India's International Economy in the Nineteenth Century: An Historical Survey," *Modern Asian Studies* 2: 1 (1968), p. 34.

12. Quoted in Y.C. Wang, "Intellectuals and Society in China 1860–1949," *Comparative Studies in Society and History* 3: 4 (July 1961), p. 410.

13. Michael Adas, "Modernization Theory and the American Revival of the Scientific and Technological Standards of Social Achievement and Human Worth," in David Engerman et al., *Staging Growth* (Boston: University of Massachusetts, 2003), p. 27.

14. On the Grimm brothers, see Linda Degh, "Grimm's 'Household Tales' and Its Place in the Household: The Social Relevance of a Controversial Classic," *Western Folklore* 38: 2 (April 1979), p. 85.

15. Joseph Pittau, "Inoue Kowashi, 1843–1895, and the Formation of Modern Japan," *Monumenta Nipponica* 20: 3/4 (1965), p. 273.

16. Ibid., p. 38.

17. Quoted in Lloyd G. Reynolds, *Economic Growth in the Third World, 1850–1980* (New Haven: Yale University, 1985), p. 20.

18. Paul Bairoch, *Economics and World History: Myths and Paradoxes* (New York: Simon & Schuster, 1993), p. 104.

19. Francois Bourguignon and Christian Morrison, "Inequality Among World Citizens: 1820–1992," *American Economic Review* 92: 4 (September 2002), p. 737.

20. Richard A. Easterlin, "The Worldwide Standard of Living Since 1800," *Journal of Economic Perspectives* 14: 1 (Winter 2000), pp. 15, 13.

21. From the *Contemporary Review*, quoted in *New York Times*, July 13, 1890, p. 19.

22. A.A. Paton, *A History of the Egyptian Revolution* (London: Trubner, 1863), p. 73.

23. Edward William Lane, *Description of Egypt*, ed. Jason Thompson (Cairo: American University, 2000), p. 146.

24. Frederic Trautmann, *With Perry to Japan: A Memoir by William Heine* (Honolulu: University of Hawaii, 1990), p. 131.

25. Meiji official quoted in Andrew Gordon, *Modern History of Japan* (New York: Oxford, 2003), p. 72.

26. Quoted in Paul Varley, *Japanese Culture* (Honolulu: University of Hawaii, 2000), p. 244.

27. Quoted in W.G. Beasley, *The Rise of Modern Japan* (London: Weidenfeld & Nicolson, 1990), p. 99.

28. Quoted in Ian Buruma, *Inventing Japan, 1853–1964* (London: Weidenfeld & Nicolson, 2003), p. 37.

29. Julie Lee Wei, Ramon Myers, and Donald Gillin, eds., *Prescriptions for Saving China: Selected Writings of Sun Yat-sen* (Stanford, CA: Hoover Institution Press, 1994), p. 4.

30. Evelyn Waugh, *Black Mischief* (New York: Little, Brown, 1960), p. 22.

31. International Labour Conference, *Forced Labour: Report and Draft Questionnaire* (Twelfth session, Geneva, 1929), p. 233.

32. *Report of the East Africa Commission* (London: His Majesty's Stationery Office, 1925), pp. 10, 22; Secretary of State for the Colonies, *Kenya: Compulsory Labour for Government Purposes* (London: His Majesty's Stationery Office, 1925), p. 9.

33. Badruddin Tyabji's 1887 presidential address to the Madras Congress, quoted in Sanjay Seth, "Rewriting Histories of Nationalism: The Politics of 'Moderate Nationalism' in India, 1870–1905," *American Historical Review* 104: 1 (February 1999), p. 103.

34. Ibid., pp. 97, 103, 106.

CHAPTER

1

Porfirio Díaz:
Importing Modernity

The most famous modernizer in Latin American history was Porfirio Díaz, the ruler of Mexico for three decades from 1876 to 1911. The Díaz years were so important that they are known in Spanish as *el Porfiriato*—the reign of Porfirio. Mexico changed rapidly during the Porfiriato, creating thousands of miles of railroad lines and hundreds of new mines, textile mills, and other large factories. The country became integrated into the world economy—its exports increased over 600 percent. At the same time, the United States became Mexico's main trading partner, and American investors poured over a billion dollars into the country. Visitors to Mexico during the Porfiriato marveled at the rapid economic changes and praised Díaz for imposing order where before bandits had ruled. "He is a Dictator," the *New York Times* declared approvingly in 1901, "who has given the Mexican people a better Government than they could have provided for themselves."[1]

Yet, in what might seem to be a great paradox, the "peace and progress" of the Porfiriato ended in bloodshed when the

Mexican Revolution erupted in 1911, forcing Díaz into exile. Before boarding a steamship, a mystified Díaz wondered why "the Mexican people . . . have risen up in armed bands, alleging that my presence . . . is the cause of their insurrection," and concluding, "I am unaware of any action of mine that could have motivated this phenomenon."[2] Although Díaz pleaded ignorance, nearly all other Mexicans understood that his program of modernization had somehow caused the Mexican Revolution. This chapter will explore the rapid changes brought on by the drive to modernize Mexico and why they led to revolution rather than prosperity and stability.

SPAIN'S JEWEL IN THE CROWN

In 1830, the year Porfirio Díaz was born, Mexico had just severed its ties to Spain after being a colony for 300 years. Unlike Japan and China, which kept Europeans out until the 19th century, Mexico had ceased to rule itself in the 1520s, when Hernán Cortés conquered the Aztecs. During three long centuries of colonial rule, many Spaniards settled in Mexico, where colonial law made them the ruling elite. Some of these Europeans, called *peninsulares* because they came from the Iberian Peninsula, married into indigenous families. Their offspring were called *mestizos*, people of mixed European and Indian ancestry.

Outside the cities and larger towns of colonial Mexico, a large part of the population remained decidedly Indian. In theory, the Indians were Spanish subjects and had to embrace Roman Catholicism. In practice, Spain accepted the fact that Indians had their own beliefs and way of life. Indian villagers chose their own leaders and owned their own lands, which they often held communally. Indians paid taxes to the Spanish government and lip service to the Church, but many lived largely as they had before Cortés arrived.

The Virgin of Guadalupe, Mexico's patron saint and even today a powerful national symbol, embodies the dual nature of Mexico. *La Virgencita*, as she is known, was an apparition of the Virgin Mary on a hill outside Mexico City in 1531. But the hill was sacred to the Aztec goddess Tonantzin, and the *Virgencita* has often been pictured as brown-skinned and Indian-featured. Roman Catholic and Indian— that was Mexico in the time of Porfirio Díaz.

RICH COLONY

Minerals made New Spain, as the Spanish called Mexico, the richest colony in Latin America. Mexico's rugged mountains held vast reserves of silver and lesser amounts of gold. By 1810, just before independence, Mexican mines were producing more than half the total world supply of silver. Mexican silver coins, called *reales*, circulated throughout the Americas and far beyond. Colonists in Virginia and other parts of British North America accepted *reales* as their basic currency, and Mexican mints even provided the most common coin in China. (The *reales* arrived through the nearby Philippines, another Spanish colony.) So, although Mexico was far away from Europe, it was not peripheral to the wealth of Spain and Europe generally. In fact, economic historians have found that when Spanish treasure fleets began to haul Mexican (and Peruvian) silver and gold across the Atlantic in the 1560s, the infusion of bullion was so great that it caused massive European-wide inflation, a phenomenon known as the Price Revolution.

Treasure fleets are not the whole story of colonial Mexico, however. Satisfied with the riches that poured from Mexico's mines, Spain did little to develop the colony in other ways. Mexico's landforms range from tropical lowlands to temperate highlands to high mountain peaks, allowing a wide variety of crops to grow. Before Cortés conquered Mexico, indigenous people raised cotton and wove it into cloth, cultivated cacao, the source of chocolate, and grew tobacco. Intent on extracting Mexico's silver and gold, Spain had little interest in encouraging those valuable crops, so their production declined. For the same reason, Spain spent little on Mexico's infrastructure beyond the primitive road system needed to extract minerals through the main port of Veracruz. Mexico, criss-crossed by mountain ranges, lacked the navigable rivers that made transportation easy in the United States (think of the Mississippi, Ohio, and Hudson rivers, for example, as well as the Great Lakes). Overcoming the obstacles to moving goods in and out of Mexico would be a major goal of the Díaz regime.

Although mines produced nearly all of Mexico's exportable wealth, most people in the colony were farmers. On the huge land grants that Spain gave to settlers, owners raised cattle, corn, wheat, and other food crops. Beyond these *haciendas*, mestizo peasants and Indian villagers raised corn, beans, and other crops to feed their families. The different regions of Mexico were largely self-sufficient "islands," producing most of life's basic necessities themselves. Even during times of famine—when a corn surplus in one area might have saved hungry peasants in another—bad roads and high transportation costs kept supplies from reaching the areas that needed them.

STRUGGLING REPUBLIC

This basic economic pattern did not change with Mexico's independence in 1821. Indeed, during the years of warfare between Spanish soldiers and Mexican patriots from 1810 to 1821, roads fell into disrepair, mines were burned or flooded, and silver exports plunged. The new Mexican government also kept the colonial *alcabalas*, internal taxes on goods that crossed from one state to another, which raised prices and discouraged trade. Mexico's economy was even more local, more limited to subsistence, than it had been as a colony.

Mexico's first years of independence were very different from the early history of the United States. The United States passed through a brief period of instability under the Articles of Confederation, but with the ratification of the Constitution in 1788 and the election of George Washington as president, Americans created a remarkably stable political order that lasted until the Civil War erupted in 1861. This was not the case in Mexico, or in the rest of Latin America, or in fact in most of the African, Asian, and Middle Eastern colonies that won independence from colonial rule in the 20th century. In most former colonies, independence brought political disorder and economic decline, not stability and steady progress.

YEARS OF CHAOS

Mexico's economic problems began almost at once. A few years after winning independence, Mexico borrowed millions of dollars in London, the world's leading capital market at the time. Mexico's leaders had a noble goal—to use the money to develop the economy, something Spain had not done during three centuries of colonial rule. Unfortunately, political turmoil and a weak central government forced Mexico to default on this early loan, barring it from getting new credit abroad for decades. With no funds to repair the ravages of the war with Spain or to build much-needed infrastructure, Mexico's economy shrank in the years after independence. Silver exports, the backbone of the traditional economy, dropped sharply after 1810. As the table shows, silver output began to climb slowly in the 1830s but did not return to the peak output of the last decade of colonial rule until the 1870s.

Mexican silver production, in kilograms

Year	Silver (kg)
1801–1810	5,538,000
1811–1820	3,120,000
1821–1830	2,648,000
1831–1840	3,309,900
1841–1850	4,203,100
1851–1860	4,569,500
1861–1870	4,969,500
1871–1880	5,831,109

Source: "La Minería," in Ciro Cardoso, ed., *México en el siglo XIX* (Mexico City: Nueva Imagen, 1980).

Political turmoil worsened Mexico's economic problems. The expulsion of Spanish officials left a power vacuum that led to fighting among rivals for the presidency. In Mexico's first 50 years of independence, more than 30 different men served as president. (By contrast, the United States had eight presidents from 1789 to 1840.) One man, General Antonio López de Santa Anna, served as president no fewer than 11 times between 1833 and 1855. Only two presidents finished their legal terms, while others held on just a few weeks before rivals drove them from office.

Political turmoil in Mexico made the country the victim of foreign intervention. Mexico's thinly populated northern provinces, including Texas, New Mexico, and California, lay directly in the path of westward expansion by the United States. In 1835, American settlers in Texas rebelled against the distant rulers in Mexico City and declared Texas a free republic (although one that allowed slavery). A decade later, the U.S. Congress made Texas a state, triggering war with Mexico. Even as American troops landed in Veracruz and marched toward Mexico City, rival Mexican leaders fought among themselves. When the war ended in 1848, the victorious Americans demanded nearly half of Mexico's territory—the vast region encompassing modern-day California, Nevada, and Utah, most of Arizona, and parts of New Mexico, Colorado, and Wyoming. The humiliating defeat and harsh peace put Mexico's survival as an independent nation in doubt.

LA REFORMA AND THE FRENCH INVASION

Twenty-five years of disorder and decline led many Mexicans to long for a new beginning. Leading the call for renewal were liberals who hoped to remake Mexico in the image of the United States. These reformers pointed out that Mexico had never really broken with its colonial past. The liberals demanded basic changes in Mexican society—what came to be known as *la Reforma*.

La Reforma took aim at three groups that enjoyed special rights and represented, according to liberals, the dead hand of the colonial past, and thus obstacles to progress: the army; the Catholic Church; and Indian communities in the countryside. Each was a distinct entity governed by special laws known as *fueros*. Neither priests nor soldiers, for example, could be brought to trial in regular courts. If charged with a crime, they faced judgment by members of their own institution in special ecclesiastical or military courts, respectively. To liberals, those special rights subverted the ideal of equality before the law and kept Mexico from being a true republic.

Liberals had more practical grievances against the army and Church as well. For decades, the army had been guilty of meddling in politics, often overthrowing elected leaders. The Catholic Church, in addition to its spiritual mission, played a dominant role in Mexico's economy. The Church owned huge amounts of the country's best land, accumulated over the centuries when pious Catholics bequeathed it their property. The Church was, in fact, the nation's largest landowner after the government. Since there were few banks in Mexico, the Church also served as a money lender. Liberals believed the Church should concern itself with spiritual matters and have less to do with the nation's economy.

Although Indians could hardly be called privileged, they were also a distinct population. In the countryside, many Indians lived in relative isolation, speaking Nahuatl, Zapoteca, Maya, and other native languages and farming the communally owned lands they had held since before the conquest. Reformers disliked the closed Indian communities and attacked the ancient practice of collective landowning, believing that small landholders were the backbone of any republic. Liberals called for privatizing the Indian lands and taking away most of the property owned by the Catholic Church, as well. By doing so they would turn Mexico's poor peasants into industrious, profit-oriented farmers and make the country's underused lands far more productive.

In the 1850s, Benito Juárez, himself a full-blooded Indian, led the liberals against the conservative government of perennial president Santa Anna. After years of fighting, the liberals finally won, and Juárez became president of Mexico in 1857. The liberals wrote a new constitution that embodied many of their ideals, ending the *fueros* for the army and Church, separating Church and state for the first time, and reducing the powers of the president in order to discourage dictatorships. The new document also stripped the Church of most of its property and required Indian communities to parcel out their collective land to individual owners. On paper, the liberals had accomplished many of their goals, but civil war over the next decade would leave most aspects of *la Reforma* a dead letter.

The liberal constitution rallied conservative supporters of the Church and army, and once more Mexico plunged into a fratricidal war. By 1861 the conservatives had lost, so they looked abroad for support. The ambitious ruler of France, Napoleon III, had long dreamed of reestablishing his nation's power in the New World. Making Mexico a French colony would violate the Monroe Doctrine, declared by the United States in 1823, but since Americans were slaughtering each other in their own civil war, Washington had no time to worry about Mexico. Mexico's default on international bonds, some of which were held by French citizens, gave Napoleon III a pretext for intervention. In 1862, French troops landed at Veracruz, marched on Mexico City, and installed Maximilian, the brother-in-law of Napoleon, as emperor of Mexico. Mexicans rose up to expel the French, and the country was once again at war.

THE RISE OF PORFIRIO DÍAZ

The nearly constant warfare from 1847 to 1867 devastated Mexico's economy, but gave ambitious young men a chance to make a name for themselves as soldiers. None seized that opportunity more fervently than Porfirio Díaz.

Born in Oaxaca (wa HA ka), a province whose population was over 90 percent indigenous at the time, Díaz grew up among Zapoteca and Mixteca Indians. Indeed, Díaz had Indian blood in his veins. (See the excerpt from his memoirs at the end of this chapter.) The liberal cause attracted Díaz—he knew and admired Benito Juárez, another Oaxacan. As a young officer, Díaz showed a gift for winning the loyal support of the Indians and mestizos that he trained as soldiers. In Oaxaca, Díaz escaped death and capture at the hands of the conservatives and won battle after battle for the liberal cause. Juárez, glad for the support of such an able young soldier, commented, "Es un buen chico, Porfirio" (Porfirio is a good kid.)[3]

Having proved himself in the struggle to bring Juárez to power, Díaz became a national hero in the battle against France. As French troops marched west from Veracruz in the spring of 1862, Díaz helped to halt their advance at the Battle of Puebla. Mexico's temporary victory over the European army on May 5 is still a national holiday— *el Cinco de Mayo*. During the battle, Díaz disobeyed his commanding officer and led an infantry division in a flanking move that took the French by surprise. "We suffered considerable losses," he admitted, "but we killed many, many *monsieurs*."[4] Díaz took credit for the victory and added to the military reputation that would be the basis of his political career. Captured twice by the French, Díaz escaped both times—once disguised as an Indian peasant, the second time by tunneling out of his cell. His exploits made him a popular legend. As we shall see again in the cases of Menelik II in Ethiopia and Mustafa Kemal in Turkey, military success against the armies of more developed nations gave modernizing leaders the prestige and public support they needed to undertake radical changes.

From his early days as a soldier, Díaz exhibited qualities that would later help him capture the presidency. The chaotic conditions in Mexico favored a leader who could think fast on his feet. "When I was first commanding troops," he recalled many years later, "there were times when I received neither orders nor supplies for months on end. I was obliged to think for myself and make myself into the government."[5] Díaz also showed early on that he had no scruples about spilling blood when it served his ends. He ordered the execution of prisoners and ruthlessly suppressed dissent. Never a gifted speaker, Díaz nevertheless projected immense power through his reserved manner—always serious, never smiling.

Observing men and women of different backgrounds during wartime gave Díaz a cynical view of human nature. "The individual who helps his country in a time of war or peace always has some personal motivation," he commented. "His ambition may be good or bad, but deep inside there is always some ambition."[6] As president, Díaz assumed that both his friends and opponents acted out of self-interest rather than patriotism or concern for the common good.

That view certainly described his own patriotism. Although Díaz fought bravely for the liberal cause, he did so with an eye to eventually making himself president. The time to act came in 1867, when Mexico finally expelled the French and a firing squad ended the imperial dreams of Maximilian. From that moment until 1876, Díaz made clear that he meant to rule Mexico, constitutionally or otherwise. He first ran for president in 1867. He tried again in 1871 and, after losing to Benito Júarez, led an armed rebellion against his old friend and liberal mentor. After Juárez died in 1872, Díaz tried and failed to overthrow the new president, Sebastián Lerdo de Tejada. Driven into exile, Díaz returned in 1876 to seize the presidency at last. Elections in 1877 confirmed him as ruler of Mexico, giving Díaz the prize he had sought so long.

DÍAZ IN POWER

Having fought his way into power, the first order of business for Díaz was to prevent further regime changes. Years of war had left the country in a state of near anarchy. For the time being, Díaz concentrated on enforcing order. He used nearly two-thirds of the national budget for the army and police. There could be no progress without peace: Mexico's very first telephone line, strung in 1879, connected Díaz to his chief of police.

To impose order in the countryside, Díaz sharpened an instrument first created by Juárez—the Rurales, or rural police force. Díaz allowed murderers and highwaymen to join the Rurales, a policy that at once reduced the number of bandits and guaranteed that the police would not be squeamish about using force. Mexicans soon found that the Rurales dispensed justice without the inconvenience of a trial. Díaz made clear that the iron fist suited him. When the governor of Veracruz warned of a group plotting against him, Díaz wired back a succinct order: "Mátalos en caliente" (Shoot them at once.)[7]

Soldiers and police who turned against the dictator could expect no mercy—their job, after all, was to keep him in power. With middle-class, urban, educated opponents, the dictator normally used gentler tactics—bribes rather than bullets. If a critic made too much noise, Díaz found him a job, gave him a lucrative contract, or offered an outright bribe, often with the comment: "Ese gallo quiere maíz" (That rooster needs some corn.) When a newspaper dared to criticize him, the dictator might promise the publisher a government subsidy or simply order the paper closed.

COATZACOALCOS   Calle Colón. Presidente Porfirio Díaz paseandose

President Porfirio Díaz, dressed in a black suit, surrounded by military officers and local officials during a walking tour of the port city of Coatzacoalos, on the Gulf of Mexico.

Until the final years of his reign, Díaz opted for a flexible approach to his opponents, a delicate balance of force and favoritism. The strategy avoided constant violence that would have rallied public opinion against him. The combination was the secret behind what came to be known as the *Pax Porfiriano*—the peace of Porfirio. One Mexican historian has called the Porfiriato a *dictablanda* rather than a *dictadura*—a play on Spanish words meaning a soft rather than hard dictatorship.

MODERNIZING MEXICO

Before Díaz, liberal leaders had focused their energy on Mexico's political problems—guaranteeing the right to vote, freedom of religion, and so on. Mexico's new president had little interest in such "abstractions." Unlike Benito Juárez, Díaz's notion of progress had little to do with elections, the constitution, or a free press but a great deal to do with railroads, exports, and keeping the peace by any means necessary. It is true that Díaz always allowed elections to take place. But since he handpicked the candidates for both houses of congress, and often for the state legislatures as well, his control of the nation was never in doubt. As Díaz said in 1881, "candidates should be more or less friends of mine."[8]

For Díaz, modernity meant economic development, not political freedom. "The power and greatness of modern nations," he declared in 1896, "is essentially rooted in their economic organization, measured by the extent of their wealth, the health of their national treasury, and the state of their public credit."[9] Díaz summed up this economic view of modernity when he quipped that Mexico's docks, where exporters shipped the nation's products abroad, mattered more than the country's laws—in Spanish, *muelles* rather than *leyes*.[10]

Díaz believed that only economic growth could firmly root the peace that had eluded Mexico for the first 50 years of independence. He agreed with Francisco Zarco, a leading liberal intellectual, who concluded, "Where there are roads and post offices, railroads and telegraphs, hospitals, schools, factories and workshops, trade and industry, peace will naturally be maintained because everyone will try to preserve it."[11]

During his first term from 1876 to 1880, however, Díaz could only take small steps toward his goal of modernizing Mexico. Peace, not progress, was his first priority. When his first term ended in 1880, Díaz left office without a fight. This was wise, since his successor, Manuel González, a loyal friend since childhood, moved forward with the Díaz agenda. In the elections of 1884, Mexicans once more put their faith in Díaz.

THE DÍAZ SYSTEM

Back in power, Díaz gradually extended personal control over Mexico's congress, court system, provincial governors, and even local officials. The dictator's phenomenal memory for names helped—it was said he could recall every one of Mexico's hundreds of congressmen. Díaz did not care about building a political party that would outlive him or a bureaucracy that could operate apart from his personal control. He made himself the center of Mexico's political and economic system, making all key decisions and even occupying himself with minor issues. He never became all-powerful, but he certainly tried.

One opposition paper, *El Monitor Republicano*, put it plainly, "Here in Mexico there is no people, there is no republic, there is no power, beyond the will of General Díaz." A pro-government editor retorted that Díaz could not be blamed for concentrating power in his own hands: "Mexico has never been governed democratically for the simple reason that the Mexican people are not democratic."[12]

Unlike some modernizers, including Mustafa Kemal and Communist leaders like Mao Zedong, Díaz did not seek to remake every aspect of Mexican society. He chose his targets carefully, focusing on economic change. He did not take on the traditional enemies of the liberals—the army and the Catholic Church. Instead, he made peace with them. He kept the armed forces relatively small but had congress pump extra money into its budget so that army officers could skim off the excess, which kept them happy and out of politics. Díaz largely ignored the Church, which, after the attacks on its privileges launched by Benito Júarez and other liberals, made the priests and the Vatican happy.

When he returned to power, Díaz found that it was a propitious moment to forge ahead with economic modernization. For the first time since independence, Mexico's government had enough money and power to snuff out both bandits and rebels. Moreover, an economic depression that had slowed world trade in the 1870s was over, and the industrialized countries once again had insatiable appetites for all sorts of raw materials, especially food crops and minerals. Díaz and his advisors understood that Mexico could remake itself as a supplier of commodities to the industrial world. Through export-driven development, Mexico would accumulate enough capital to build the infrastructure needed for a modern economy. The country could even begin the process of industrialization. Mexico, they dreamed, would follow the path that England and the United States had blazed, emerging as a modern, industrial nation.

By the early 1890s, Díaz left the details of economic policy to a group of young modernizers known as the *científicos,* or scientists, who claimed they would apply the latest ideas of the social sciences to Mexican development. Chief among them was José Yves Limantour, the secretary of finance, who balanced Mexico's budget for the first time since independence. Limantour also eliminated the *alcabalas* in order to promote trade inside Mexico.

The most respected economic theory of the time was *laissez-faire,* a French term that meant governments should let private initiative direct the economy. But that theory was of little use if Mexico hoped to catch up with Western Europe and the United States. So although the *científicos* paid lip service to laissez-faire, they used the government aggressively to modernize Mexico.

PREMODERN MEXICO

The nation that Díaz hoped to modernize was underdeveloped even by Latin American standards. Argentina, Brazil, and Chile had built thousands of kilometers of railroad by the 1870s, while Mexico had managed only to lay a few hundred kilometers. Mexico's first railroad, a relatively short link between the capital and Veracruz, had been planned in the 1830s but was not completed until 1873. That early line followed the same winding mule trails that Spain had used to extract silver and gold from the colony in the old days. It did little to open the country's vast interior to commerce.

If Mexico's exports lagged far behind those of Argentina and Brazil, the lack of efficient, low-cost transportation was a key reason. Mexican economic historian Paolo Riguzzi argues that even in the 1870s Mexico had not fully entered the age of iron and the wheel, given that mules and human carriers still hauled many goods.[13] In 1897 the *New York Times* called Mexico's transportation system "prehistoric" and described men who "carry on their backs, clear to the City of Mexico, the crops of great haciendas far back in the mountains."[14]

Poor transportation was not the only obstacle to Mexico's development. Economic historian Stephen Haber notes that as late as the 1880s "almost all of the features which permitted industrial growth to occur rapidly in the Western European and United States settings were lacking in Mexico."[15] These features included productive, export-oriented agriculture, adequate legal protections for property, political stability, a robust home market for consumer goods, a system of banks that made capital easily available, and low entry costs for manufacturers. Clearly, modernizing Mexico would be no easy task.

Economic data do not capture the true state of Mexico after decades of war. As late as the 1890s, nearly half of all babies born in Mexico died before their first birthday. The comparable statistic in Boston at the time was one in ten. Even in 1910, average life expectancy in Mexico hovered around 30 years, while most U.S. inhabitants at the time could expect to reach 50. The Mexican government reported the same year that nearly half the houses in Mexico were shacks, better suited to shelter farm animals than people.

Poverty underlay these dismal statistics. Wealthy Mexicans complained that the poor lived in utter filth. But since peasants and unskilled workers earned an average of only 1 peso a day, a poor family would have had to spend nearly 25 percent of their weekly income just to buy soap.[16] Lectures and newspaper stories on good hygiene could never overcome that brutal reality.

RAILROADS: TOUCHSTONES OF MODERNITY

To modernizers like Díaz, the key to transforming Mexico was the railroad. It is difficult for us to comprehend how, in the epoch before cars, airplanes, and computers, rail lines promised to revolutionize premodern societies. The countryside remained backward, modernizers assumed, because it was prohibitively costly for peasants to ship goods to market. That single fact explained why so many peasants grew just enough food for the families rather than raising cash crops. The cost of shipping coffee or cotton on mules, wooden carts, or the backs of human carriers erased any profit they might earn.

The railways changed everything. Railroads reduced the cost of shipping by 90 percent, so farmland used by peasant families to raise corn and beans could now be irrigated, fertilized, and worked intensively to raise export crops. But gleaming, steam-driven trains did much more than lower freight costs. Railroads knit together regions that before had little contact. They carried mail and newspapers to the countryside, teaching peasants about the outside world. They also allowed the government to send the Rurales or soldiers to chase bandits and put down rebellions. Díaz stated frankly that the steel of the rails would "complete the work begun by steel bayonets—the conquest of national unity."[17]

Mexico had so few railroads in part because of its proximity to the United States. Mexican leaders worried that railways would bind them to their northern neighbor, well on its way to becoming the world's most dynamic industrial nation. Would not Mexico then become an annex of the United States, the impoverished supplier of raw materials to ravenous factories across the Rio Grande? Mexican leaders before Díaz assumed so and rejected the railroad. President Lerdo de Tejada had said, "Entre la fuerza y la debilidad, el desierto," (Between strength and weakness, leave the desert.)[18]

Despite fears about Americans controlling Mexico's economy, in the end Díaz gave contracts for three major trunk lines to U.S. companies. The firms laid track at a speed that astonished Mexicans, but the results were predictable. Each of the American companies had agreed to build lines from west to east, connecting the Pacific Coast to the

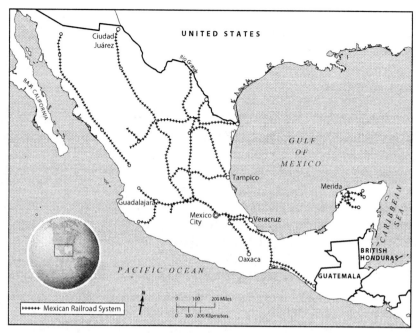

The railroad system built during the Porfiriato connected Mexico to the booming industrial economy of its northern neighbor.

Gulf of Mexico. All three ignored those promises and poured resources into completing the north–south routes that linked Mexico to the American rail system. As the map shows, by the mid-1880s Mexico had three major lines connecting it to the United States, but it still had no way to ship goods from one coast to the other. Not surprisingly, the opening of the trunk lines resulted in a steady increase in Mexican trade with the United States and a steady decline in exports to and imports from Europe. In 1877, Great Britain bought 35 percent of Mexico's exports. By 1910, Britain's share had fallen to 12 percent, while the U.S. share had grown from 42 to 76 percent.[19]

THE AMERICAN CONNECTION

Díaz and his circle understood that their country lacked the wealth and technical skill needed to build the vast new projects they planned— railroads, ports, and bridges; telegraph, telephone, and electrical systems; lead smelters, iron foundries, and textile mills. "Lacking as we do both the men and the money necessary for the full development of the manifold resources of our soil," Limantour admitted, "we are not in a position to reject those elements when offered to us, simply because they come from other lands."[20] At first, the capital and technology Mexico needed came from Europe. By the 1890s, however, the United States played the leading role in Mexico's push toward modernity.

Díaz and his various ambassadors to Washington courted wealthy Americans to invest in their country's mines, plantations, factories, railroads, and infrastructure. The dictator invariably found time to meet personally with Americans who traveled to Mexico. Díaz was "well thought of by resident foreigners," the *New York Times* reported, "especially by Americans, for he has always . . . been a bulwark of protection to foreign interests." It was precisely "the feeling of security that he inspires that attracts and keeps foreign capital in Mexico," the paper noted.[21]

During the Porfiriato, the American colony in Mexico grew from a small nucleus to over 10,000, the largest settlement of expatriate Americans in Latin America. Americans published the Mexican *Herald* and other English-language newspapers to promote U.S. investment in Mexico. Díaz appreciated the publicity and proved it by giving the *Herald* a healthy subsidy. Some advisors to the dictator married wealthy American women, who took up residence in Mexico City and provided useful contacts back in the States.

After 1900, the pace of U.S. investment in Mexico increased dramatically, and Díaz realized that many of his countrymen resented the American presence. Foreigners seemed to have more rights than Mexicans did. Critics lamented that Mexico was the mother of foreigners and the stepmother of her own people. Díaz and his advisors tried to lure European investors to counterbalance the growing American role, but that did little to change the impression that Díaz had sold Mexico out to foreign capitalists.

EXPORTS VERSUS INDIANS

The liberal constitution of 1857 had called for the communal lands of the Indians to be divided into private farms. In the turbulent years before Díaz became president, the Indians had largely resisted the policy. Díaz and his advisors believed self-sufficient peasants did little to help Mexico's economy. To make Mexican agriculture more productive, Díaz pushed aggressively to wrest land away from Indians and poor mestizos. The instrument he used was private land companies, empowered to keep one-third of all the land they surveyed. Legally, the companies could only survey *terrenos baldíos*—unused lands owned by the government. In practice, they brazenly took over Indian lands, knowing full well that was the president's wish.

The land companies privatized approximately 96 million acres of land during the Porfiriato. The result was an astonishing concentration of landownership. By 1910, land held communally by Indians had dropped to a mere 5 percent of national territory. The official figures showing who took over the land are even more amazing. Privatization was allegedly intended to create millions of small farms worked by industrious families. The reality was that by 1910 less than 2 percent of Mexico's population owned *all* its legally titled farmland. The overwhelming majority of Mexicans continued to live as farmers, yet 90 percent of them owned no land at all. Instead, they toiled as farm laborers for meager wages on large haciendas and plantations, although the word *large* pales before the reality. In Colima, three enormous haciendas engrossed a third of the state's land. In Chihuahua, the family of Luis Terrazas owned nearly 5 million acres. In practice, privatization had resulted in the transfer of millions of acres from the poorest to the wealthiest Mexicans.

It was certainly true that the land policy of Díaz moved Mexican agriculture away from subsistence and toward production for the world market. Huge haciendas, unlike tiny family plots, did produce export crops. The uptick in agricultural exports was impressive. For the first time, gold and silver no longer dominated Mexico's exports.

But the corollary of the surge in exports was a decline in food crops. Although Mexico's population nearly doubled from 1875 to 1910, the quantity of corn, wheat, and beans grown actually went down over the same period. Corn production fell from 2.5 million tons in 1877 to under 2 million tons in 1910.[22] The reason was straightforward: Land once used to grow food crops was now dedicated to export production. Moreover, Mexico actually exported more of this smaller production of foodstuffs. Because Mexico was raising less food for more people, food prices moved up sharply, resulting in malnutrition for many of the rural poor.

Like so many other policies of the Díaz regime, the country's progress in exports came at the expense of the Mexican people. The científicos who designed Mexican economic policy could proudly point to statistics showing huge increases in export earnings. But those profits went to the owners of large haciendas, plantations, and mines, many of whom were foreigners, not Mexicans. In the countryside, Mexicans saw land torn from Indian communities and swallowed by land companies. The vast majority who worked in the blazing sun on someone else's land for a peso a day could find little to celebrate in Mexico's progress. On average, they earned lower wages and paid more for food than they had 30 years earlier.

INDIANS AND IMMIGRANTS

A few members of Mexico's political and economic elite objected to the expropriation of Indian lands. Most, however, saw the process as an inevitable step in Mexico's evolution toward modernity. In keeping with a simplified version of Charles Darwin's idea of "the survival of the fittest," many educated Mexicans assumed that the Indians were on the road to extinction. The government could not, and should not try, to save them.

To replace the "vanishing" Indians, elite Mexicans called on the government to attract more immigrants from Europe. In the United States, they pointed out, millions of immigrant workers toiled in factories, in mines, and on railroads. Why not bring more of these hardworking, light-skinned men and women to Mexico? Government officials agreed and offered tempting incentives to newcomers from Europe.

Ultimately, however, low wages and harsh working conditions kept most European immigrants from choosing Mexico as a destination. In 1895, about 50,000 foreigners lived in Mexico; by 1910, the number had grown only to about 120,000. By contrast, in the single year 1905, over a million immigrants entered the United States; in the decade from 1901 to 1910, over 8 million newcomers arrived. Immigrants would not be Mexico's salvation.

INDUSTRIALIZING MEXICO

Although the científicos pushed Mexico to produce export crops, they were not content to make their nation a mere supplier to the industrial world of sugar cane, henequen, copper, and lead. Recent work by Stephen Haber and Edward Beatty shows that Díaz and his advisors actively tried to foster industry. One policy gave concessions to companies that introduced new industries into the nation. Concessions offered tax reductions and other benefits to capitalists who agreed to invest a large sum in an industry that was entirely new to Mexico. A more effective policy was to reduce import taxes—tariffs—on goods needed for industrial growth, such as machinery and raw cotton, while keeping tariffs relatively high on finished products like foods and clothing. By manipulating the tariff, Mexico achieved what economists call *import-substitution industrialization,* or ISI. ISI meant raising import tariffs high enough on basic manufactured goods—clothing, tools, glass, cement, paper, food, beer, and so on—so that local factories could produce the goods more cheaply.

The policy worked. Factories supplying simple consumer needs sprouted up, especially in central Mexico. By 1901, Mexico City had 22 textile mills, 15 chemical plants, 34 brickyards, 7 shoe factories, and many other industrial firms producing basic products for the domestic market. Economic historian Edward Beatty notes that the large-scale, capital-intensive industries that grew after 1890 would not have been profitable without tariff protection. By 1910, imports made up less than half of basic consumer goods—the balance was supplied by local manufacturers.[23]

As happened in other branches of industry, Mexico developed large-scale breweries during the Porfiriato. As local production increased after 1890, imports of foreign beers declined sharply. By 1900 five large national companies, including the Moctezuma brewery shown here, dominated Mexico's beer market.

Like the export boom, creating new industries made modernizers happy. For them, the factories that poured out tools, iron, chemicals, and cotton cloth proved that Mexico had left behind its colonial past and was rapidly evolving into a modern nation. But ordinary Mexicans saw things differently. Factories produced goods cheaply—that was the whole reason for building them. Yet in Mexico locally made goods were expensive because factory owners did not have to worry about underselling imports. Once again, a policy that improved Mexico's macroeconomic posture made life harder for the poor majority.

THE NEW ECONOMY BREEDS UNREST

If consumers were unhappy, Mexico's factory workers had even more reason to be discontent. Working conditions in factories were abominable. Workers in textile mills toiled at their machines for more than 12 hours a day. Owners made low wages even lower by docking workers' pay for any "defective" products they turned out. They fired workers injured by dangerous machinery. In remote mining areas, workers sweated underground day in and day out only to receive their pay in chits—"money" they could use only in the company store, which not surprisingly charged high prices.

Mexican workers responded with walkouts and strikes. In some of the incidents, the demands of miners and factory workers went beyond wages and hours and challenged the Díaz regime itself. The mission of the Rurales changed accordingly. From guarding train lines and intimidating country people, they were reassigned to the factories that now dotted the landscape in central Mexico. Their purpose was clear—support the factory owners and repress any workers foolhardy enough to demand higher wages or a shorter workday.

EDUCATING THE MASSES

Perhaps the Mexican people would have endured these hardships quietly had they believed that their children would have better lives. As a liberal at least in name, Díaz often spoke about improving the condition of the Mexican masses. For decades, liberal thinkers had called for better schools as one important way to keep that promise. "The diffusion of knowledge . . . is a matter of life or death for a nation that is ruled by democratic institutions," the dictator declared.[24] At first, the educational record of the Porfiriato seems impressive. During the Díaz years, the number of grade schools doubled, and more than five times as many children went to school by the end of the period as had in the mid-1870s.

A closer look reveals that the Díaz policy in education benefited the wealthy and privileged far more than ordinary Mexicans. Díaz spent almost nothing on grade schools, the ones that mattered most to the poor. The annual budget of 7 pesos per pupil was less than 10 percent of what American states spent for primary education. But for high schools, which at the time only the children of wealthy families attended, Mexico spent *more* than the United States did.[25] Public education did little to create economic opportunity or upward mobility for the poor majority, but did provide excellent secondary schools for the elite.

TOWARD THE REVOLUTION

"There will be no revolutions while he is President of Mexico," the *New York Times* had written of Díaz in 1899.[26] But by 1906, the rumblings of a coming revolution were audible in Mexico. Many factors conspired to stoke the discontent. When miners at an American firm in northern Mexico dared to go on strike in 1906, the government's response was swift and brutal. Many strikers died, and Díaz even allowed U.S. troops to cross the border to help put down the strike. That violation of their nation's sovereignty outraged many Mexicans. A strike at a textile plant in Orizaba was also brutally repressed. Díaz admitted that "we were very hard, at times approaching cruelty. It was better to spill a little blood to prevent greater bloodshed. The blood we spilled was bad, while the blood we spared was good."[27] That was not of course the opinion of the Indian families, factory workers, and miners who suffered violence at the hands of the regime.

A sharp economic downturn in 1907 made the ordinarily hard times even worse for peasants and workers. Then, in 1908, Díaz tolled the bell for his own demise. In an interview with an American journalist, the dictator announced he would not run for reelection in 1910. At once, an anti-reelectionist movement sprang up, led by Francisco Madero. Díaz tried to backpedal, but it was too late. As challenges to the regime erupted across Mexico, Díaz used an iron fist to prove that he was in control. The political order, which for years had been flexible and canny, now revealed itself to be rigid and thus fragile.

Especially after 1900, the gap between Mexico's dream of progress and the harsh reality grew wider. During the Porfiriato, ordinary Mexicans saw signs of modernity all around them—railroads, factories, telephones, electric lights—but in their daily lives they faced grinding poverty and, in many cases, standards of living that trended down, not up. Modernization by definition brings conflict between old and new— between artisans, for example, and the factories that undermine their livelihoods. The more entrenched the traditions, and the more external the forces of change, the more likely it is that the modernization process will not be peaceful. At a certain point, many Mexicans came to feel that even disorder was better than the status quo under the sclerotic, rigidly hierarchical, and highly exclusive order of the Porfiriato.

Looking closely at what modernization under Díaz meant, we can understand why 35 years of "peace and progress" exploded in violent revolution. The Mexican Revolution that began in 1911 was not the replacement of one dictator by another, as in the pre-Porfiriato years. Instead it was a full-blown social revolution that convulsed the nation for a decade and left perhaps 1 million dead. Díaz fled the country in 1911, died in exile, and was buried in Paris in 1915. José Yves Limantour, leader of the científicos, eulogized Díaz as "the creator of modern Mexico."[28] Given the overwhelming opposition to Díaz that broke across the land like a tidal wave in 1911, it seems clear that a majority of Mexicans disagreed. In recent years, scholars have emphasized the very real economic development that Díaz brought about. Nevertheless, in his own land the reputation of Díaz has not been rehabilitated. The popular verdict is perhaps best illustrated by the fact that since the dictator's death nearly 100 years ago no Mexican government has dared to bring his remains home from Paris to be buried in his native land.

SOURCES

■ **Porfirio Díaz, Memorias**

By 1890 Porfirio Díaz had been president of Mexico for over a decade and was well known to newspaper readers in the United States and Europe. Not all the publicity about him was favorable, so his advisers urged Díaz to write his autobiography. Díaz dictated the two volumes, which were first published in a limited edition in 1892–1893, while he was still in office.

Keeping in mind that his intention is to make a favorable impression, what does Díaz emphasize about his early years? What tone does he employ, and why? What personal qualities does the "shoemaking incident" reveal? Do you think that the policies of Díaz as president of Mexico broke faith with his humble origin and upbringing?

I was born in the city of Oaxaca on September 15, 1830. . . . Although my father was partly of Spanish origin, he was in fact a *mestizo*, that is, with some mixture of Indian blood. . . . My father was a blacksmith and veterinarian by trade. . . . When he married, around 1808, he was the employee of a mineral company that had mining lands in the area . . . belonging to the cathedral of Oaxaca; later the Church leased these lands to an English company and in the end . . . Don Miguel Castro took them over in keeping with the reform laws that nationalized all the property of the Church. . . .

The well-being of my family ended when my father died in 1833 during an outbreak of cholera. I was just two years and a few months old. My mother used what little inheritance my father had left to feed me and my brothers and sisters and pay for our education. . . . When I was six she sent me to grade school . . . where they taught children to read and little else. Afterwards I went to the municipal school where I learned to write, insofar as they taught writing in those days, which is to say badly. In fact it was only later, when we were almost men, that we actually started to learn . . . At the time the requirements to graduate from secondary school were two years of Latin and three years of philosophy. . . .

One day in 1846 during the war with the United States[29] my logic teacher . . . completely ignored our topic for the day and talked to us

Source: From Porfirio Díaz, *Memorias de Porfirio Díaz*, vol. 1 (México: El Libro Francés, 1922–23), translated by Cyrus Veeser.

instead about our duty to take up arms, offering ourselves as soldiers to defend our nation against the foreign invader. He spoke so long and eloquently that when the class ended some of us marched over to the governor's office to enlist. "What the devil did you all do to get sent over here?" the governor demanded. We answered that it was a spontaneous reaction because of the situation our country was in. He had someone take down our names, and later when they organized battalions we were placed in one of them. But we never did any service other than drilling on holidays, patrolling and standing guard from time to time. . . .

My early years were more or less like those of other young men and were not marked by any remarkable incident. I was under the influence of the times I lived in . . . I felt great enthusiasm for liberal principles when I learned about them, and I felt a strong attraction for the military when I began to serve as a soldier. I was never a very good student of Latin, but I was much better at philosophy. . . . My most noteworthy qualities were that I was tall, strong and agile; I loved sports and was good at them. . . .

As time went on it became more and more difficult for my mother to sustain the family. . . . In order to help out, I began to do some manual labor, beginning by learning to make shoes for my family. The shoemaker . . . had his workshop across from my school, and during my free time I went over to chat and watch him work. Later I bought some tools and began to work on shoes in my home. One day the shoemaker came to see me. When he saw that I had some of the tools of his trade there, he asked who was making shoes. I said that I was, and he asked who had taught me the craft. I answered that he had, and explained how I had learned by watching him work. He looked at my work and although he found some defects with it, overall he said it was good. . . .

Later, when I was studying law, there was a change in the national government . . . The new government was entirely conservative and began persecuting liberals and lawyers in particular. That policy, along with the fact that I had already been trained as a soldier years earlier during the war with the United States, and the liberal ideas that I had learned . . . made me decide to become an enemy of the government.

■ Mexico through American Eyes

As American trade with, and investment in, Mexico surged after 1890, the U.S. government viewed the growing ties between the two nations as entirely positive. Indeed, government publications like the one excerpted below encouraged Americans to do business with Mexico.

How much credit does the report give to Americans for Mexico's "progress"? What are the leading areas of U.S. investment? Why might U.S. companies have had expertise in those areas? Would you expect the report to reflect concern about working conditions in Mexico's factories and mines or the overall standard of living in that country? Explain.

The amount of United States capital invested in México by 1,117 United States companies, firms, and individuals, is, in round numbers, $500,000,000 gold. This amount has practically all been invested in the past quarter century, and about one-half of it has been invested within the past five years.

The impetus given to México's industries by this enormous augmentation of the nation's working capital accounts in no small degree for the great industrial progress which it has made during the past twenty-five years. With México buying 58 per cent of all her imports from the United States and selling 80 per cent of all her exports to the United States, and with this enormous investment of United States capital in México, the commercial bond between the sister Republics is one that hardly can be broken, and is constantly growing in strength. The flow of United States capital into this Republic has apparently only begun, as each year México buys more from and sells more to the United States. . . .

More United States capital is invested in the railroads of México than in any other single line [of business]—about 70 per cent of the total. The Mexican Central Railroad represents the largest single United States interest in México. . . . The Mexican National is the next strongest. . . .

Next in importance to the railroads, from the standpoint of United States capital invested, is the mining industry. . . . A large amount . . . is invested in up-to-date mining machinery, which is competently handled, and México's mineral wealth has been greatly increased by this United States investment.

Agriculture comes after mining in the amount of United States capital invested . . . Next to railroads, mining, and agriculture, the largest United States interest in México is in manufacturing, in which United States capital is only beginning to assume importance. A number of important manufacturing enterprises, in which United States capital is heavily interested, are just starting or have plants in course of construction, as the large iron and steel works in Monterey. . . .

United States capital is also beginning to assume importance in the banking of México, and this interest is one that is growing rapidly. Next after banks, in the order of the amount of United States capital

Source: International Bureau of the American Republics, *Mexico* (Washington, DC, 1904).

invested, come assay offices and chemical laboratories, ore buyers, ore testers, smelters, and refiners, all closely allied to the mining interest. All of México's large smelters are operated by United States capital.

United States firms have of late been building many electric light and power plants, gas plants, waterworks plants, telephone systems, and similar plants. . . . In addition to building plants for their own operation, United States firms are building most of the telegraph and telephone lines and laying most of the cables for native and other foreign companies. Many of México's cities have recently undertaken or are now planning extensive municipal improvements, and in all of these the United States contractor is a conspicuous figure.

■ A Científico Analyzes the Porfiriato

Francisco Bulnes, a prominent Mexican intellectual and one of the científicos, held a number of important positions in the government of Porfirio Díaz. Something of a renegade, Bulnes dared to criticize the dictator while he was in power and defend him after he had fled.

The excerpt below reflects this dual viewpoint. What aspects of the Porfiriato does Bulnes praise? Are the accomplishments he cites primarily economic or political? What errors does he say led to the downfall of Díaz? On balance, does Bulnes see Díaz's presidency as positive or negative for Mexico?

A fact which no one can doubt or deny is that during the dictatorship of General Díaz twenty thousand kilometers of railways were constructed in Mexico, subsidized by the Government to the amount of 170,000,000 pesos silver, or $80,000,000, an average of $4,250 per kilometer. . . .

The construction work at the port of Vera Cruz, which cost 33,000,000 pesos silver, is also well known to the world. . . . The City of Mexico owes everything to the dictatorship of General Díaz. Floods formerly inundated the city every year during the rainy

Source: Francisco Bulnes, *The Whole Truth about Mexico* (New York: M. Bulnes Book Co., 1916).

season, plagues scourged it, and most unsanitary conditions prevailed, owing to the scarcity of water for the greater part of the year. Under the dictatorship a splendid system of sewers was built; water was brought from the springs of Xochimilco, and distributed according to the most scientific modern methods; streets were well paved and good pavements were laid. All this cost only 26,000,000 pesos or $13,000,000.

Under the same régime splendid buildings were erected in the City of Mexico. Among these may be mentioned the Opera House, not yet completed, which would have competed in magnificence with the Grand Opera of Paris; the Law Courts building, also in course of construction, the Post Office building, undoubtedly one of the finest buildings in the world; the General Hospital; the Insane Asylum; the Department of Railways building, classic and refined in its style of architecture. . . . Besides the sums devoted to luxurious buildings destined for political and administrative purposes, several million pesos were devoted to the construction of training-schools for teachers. . . . Without taking into consideration works of minor importance which were carried out under the dictatorship, it has been amply proved that the enormous sum of 419,000,000 pesos silver was distributed in works that were well worth while. . . .

Without renewal there is decay, and decay leads to the grave. General Díaz's ideal was the petrification of the State. He had permitted himself to be led into the irreparable error of fearing any change in the personnel of his immediate political entourage . . . The consequence was that society, seeing that a death's-head had taken the place of the living man, was shaken out of its usual tranquil mode of life . . .

In 1910 General Díaz was eighty years old. Of the eight Cabinet members, two were past eighty and the youngest was fifty-five. Of twenty state governors, two were past eighty, six past seventy, seventeen past sixty and the youngest was forty-six. The Senate was an asylum for gouty decrepits, and the House of Representatives, which ought to have vibrated with youthful vigor and activity, was composed of a host of veterans, relieved by a group of patriarchs. One of the newspapers called the Government offices the "Pyramids of Egypt, joined to the Pyramids of Teotihuacan," because of the number of mummies they contained. Such an administration could not be called progressive, not even conservative; it was a home for the aged, with a standing account at the druggist. The younger generation was justified in wanting to expel the hordes of fossils which had fastened upon the public posts as trilobites of old upon the rocks.

◼ DÍAZ CAMPAIGN IMAGE

This campaign postcard supported the reelection of Porfirio Díaz as president in 1904. For the first time, a vice president would serve alongside Díaz, which some took as a signal that Díaz was at last looking ahead to an eventual successor.

Which images on the card suggest material progress and movement toward the future? Why would the Díaz campaign include Mexico City's main cathedral, shown on the right? The eagle eating the snake in the center of the card refers to a myth about the founding of Tenochtitlan, the Aztec capital that became Mexico City after the Spanish conquest. What was the propaganda value of that image?

NOTES

1. "Diaz and Mexico," *New York Times*, June 16, 1901, p. SM9.
2. Quoted in Enrique Krauze, *Místico de la autoridad: Porfirio Díaz* (Mexico City: Fondo de Cultura Económica, 1987), pp. 135–136.
3. Ibid., p. 19.
4. Ibid., p. 16.

5. Ibid., p. 15.

6. Ibid., p. 79.

7. Quoted in Paul Garner, *Porfirio Díaz* (London: Longman, 2001), p. 87.

8. Ibid., p. 81.

9. Porfirio Díaz, *Informe del Ciudadano General Porfirio Díaz, Presidente de los Estados Unidos Mexicanos, a sus Compatriotas* (Mexico City: Imprenta del Gobierno, 1896).

10. Quoted in Krauze, *Místico*, p. 31.

11. Ibid., p. 30.

12. Ibid., p. 61.

13. Paolo Riguzzi, "Los Caminos del Atraso," in Enrique Cárdenas, ed., *Historia Económica de México* (Mexico City: Fondo de Cultura Económica, 1990), pp. 502–505.

14. "Burden Bearers in Mexico," *New York Times*, May 30, 1897, p. 16.

15. Stephen Haber, "Assessing the Obstacles to Industrialisation: The Mexican Economy, 1830–1940," *Journal of Latin American Studies* 24: 1 (February 1992), p. 3.

16. Charles C. Cumberland, *Mexico: The Struggle for Modernity* (New York: Oxford, 1968), pp. 191–192.

17. Díaz, *Informe*, p. 97.

18. Quoted in Krauze, *Místico*, p. 29.

19. Cumberland, *Mexico*, p. 228.

20. Quoted in Edward Beatty, *Institutions and Investment: The Political Basis of Industrialization in Mexico before 1911* (Stanford, CA: Stanford University, 2001), p. 34.

21. "Diaz and Mexico," *New York Times*, June 16, 1901, p. SM9.

22. Cumberland, *Mexico*, p. 204.

23. Beatty, *Institutions and Investment*, pp. 78–80.

24. Díaz, *Informe*, p. 49.

25. Cumberland, *Mexico*, pp. 233–236.

26. "The President of Mexico," *New York Times*, May 14, 1899, p. 13.

27. Krauze, *Místico*, p. 32.

28. Quoted in Garner, *Porfirio Díaz*, p. 9.

29. The Mexican-American War, 1846–1848.

Menelik II:
Africa's Modernizing Lion

In the late 1800s, Europe swallowed Africa. The growth of Europe's power and global ambition put Africa, which until the 1870s had largely escaped colonization, squarely in the sights of imperialists. In particular, the newly unified nations of Germany and Italy hoped to get a share of the colonial spoils that other European powers had long monopolized. By 1900, nearly all of sub-Saharan African had passed under European domination.

Ethiopia was the great exception to Europe's land grab in Africa, and Menelik II was the leader who kept Ethiopia free of foreign control. The story of Ethiopia under Menelik is that of an ancient civilization fighting European power at high tide. When Italy tried to take Ethiopia by force in the 1890s, Menelik inflicted the single greatest defeat by an African nation on a European power.

Even as a young man, Menelik had seen the need to unify and modernize Ethiopia. His success earned him the title "the Lion of Africa," and visitors from Europe and the United States flocked to his capital. In 1903, President Theodore Roosevelt sent a diplomatic mission to sign a trade treaty with Ethiopia. Robert Skinner, the leader of the mission, found the Ethiopian emperor to be a fascinatingly complex figure. "No king on the planet," Skinner wrote,

> has any keener appreciation of the relative forces of the earth. He has heard of Japan, and in his own way is trying to emulate that striking example. The new railroad, the new highways, the bridges, the telephones—all these things he probably cares very little for in themselves, but he realizes that nations must advance or they must fall. He wishes to lift his people up to the point of being able to comprehend and utilize these modern improvements and inventions, and to turn them to their own advantage, for the defence of their country and their national liberty.[1]

Skinner correctly understood that Menelik was not concerned about triggering an industrial revolution in the Ethiopian highlands. He did care about forging a united front against the European powers that were chipping away at Africa, and he knew that he needed substantial military power to defend his nation's independence. How he did so in the face of overwhelming odds is the focus of this chapter.

AN ANCIENT PEOPLE

The child who became Menelik II was born in 1844 into the ruling family of Shoa, a kingdom within Ethiopia ruled by his grandfather, Sahle Sellasie. Menelik's parents had great expectations for their son. By naming him Menelik, they invoked the legendary founder of Ethiopia thousands of years earlier, from whom the family claimed descent. According to tradition, the earlier Menelik was the son of King Solomon of Israel and the Queen of Sheba.

Like Porfirio Díaz, Menelik came of age in an era of near anarchy. Ethiopia was a loosely united empire made up of semi-independent kingdoms, each ruled by an aristocrat called a ras. Without a strong central government, the kingdoms often battled for power, with each ras trying to retain his territory and capture more from his rivals.

Ethiopia, or Abyssinia as Europeans called it, had a long and continuous cultural history. Located in the towering highlands between the Nile River and the Red Sea, Ethiopia is a natural fortress that historically kept out invaders and enemies. A European traveler in the 1800s described passing through the burning desert near the Red Sea and climbing into "the green and lovely highlands of Abyssinia," which he found to be a solid blanket of "rich and thriving cultivation."[2]

The core of modern Ethiopia and the heartland of Menelik's empire were these same "Christian highlands." There, about the time that the Roman Empire adopted Christianity as the state religion in the 4th century, Christianity was also accepted as the royal religion. The Ethiopian language, Amharic, is related to biblical Hebrew. The Ethiopians held on to their Christian faith even as neighboring peoples—including those of present-day Egypt, Sudan, and Somalia—converted to Islam.

Abyssinia had little contact with Europe before the opening of the Suez Canal in 1869. The canal connected the Mediterranean to the Red Sea, making a short cut around Africa for European ships headed for India and the Far East. Almost overnight the lands near the Red Sea became easily accessible and strategically important. Menelik would rise to power in exactly the years that Europe first took notice of Ethiopia.

AN AMBITIOUS KING

Menelik's father ruled Shoa from 1847 until 1855, when the kingdom was conquered by Emperor Theodore II (ca. 1818–1868), who was forcibly unifying Ethiopia. Menelik's father died during that struggle, and Theodore brought the 11-year-old boy to live with him. Menelik blamed Theodore for his father's death but admitted that the emperor "always loved me as a son; he educated me with the greatest care."[3] At Theodore's court the teenaged Menelik met visitors from across Ethiopia and beyond, including Europeans. Menelik's grasp of the "great game," the competition among Europe's Great Powers for control over less-developed peoples, began at Theodore's court.

Menelik was scarcely 20 years old when Theodore lost control of Shoa. Slipping away from Theodore's court in the night, Menelik returned home, declared himself king of Shoa, a land his family had ruled for generations, and rallied an army to his side. He won support by forgiving his defeated enemies and by allowing Islam, the other major religion in Shoa, to be practiced freely. Menelik referred to himself as the Negus Negasti, Amharic for "King of Kings," and maneuvered to become emperor of all Ethiopia.

APPROPRIATING EUROPEAN POWER

From an early age, Menelik appreciated the power of European technology. As king, he came into regular contact with Europeans, some of them charlatans who presented him with grand schemes for modernizing Ethiopia. In the 1870s, a French businessman offered "to introduce to Shoa our industry and our civilization, to assist . . . by all moral and material means to rejuvenate Ethiopia." The young king reacted with enthusiasm: "You have fathered my most secret desires."[4] The Frenchman no doubt expected to control a "rejuvenated" Ethiopia himself, with some help from Paris. Despite his fascination with all things European, however, Menelik was clear about what French "civilization" had to offer: above all, guns and ammunition.

Menelik wanted modern weapons to balance the growing power of Europeans in East Africa. By the 1870s, France and Italy were competing to control the Red Sea coast from Eritrea to Djibouti. As Britain's main imperial rival, France was happy to thwart the British in any way possible. Russia also claimed a special role in the area since Ethiopian Christians were, like the Russians, neither Roman Catholic nor Protestant but traced their faith to ancient eastern Mediterranean roots.

The Italians were the most aggressive actors in East Africa. They had established a foothold along the Red Sea in 1870 and moved steadily inland toward Menelik's kingdom, declaring their control of Eritrea, northeast of Ethiopia, in 1885. When Italy learned that the French were selling guns to Menelik, it sent its own diplomats to Shoa. Like the stream of Europeans who followed them, they were surprised by Menelik's knowledge of Europe and his wide-ranging curiosity. The king was "a fanatic for weapons," one of the Italians commented, and showed "great intelligence and great mechanical ability," according to another.[5]

Menelik learned as much as he could about the latest technology, from telephones and phonographs to movie projectors and automobiles. When an English visitor invited Menelik to London, the monarch replied, "I have heard much of your ships and your manufactures and your inventions. . . . if I went to England I should find many useful things, by bringing which to this country much good might be done."[6] Menelik's curiosity made him an effective ruler. Besides getting advice from his counselors "he also receives minute reports from all quarters, questions many persons, and even converses with children and pages, listens to everything, weighs and compares what he hears," a French aristocrat reported after meeting the emperor.[7]

As more Europeans arrived in Ethiopia, Menelik perfected the tactic of playing one against the other to his own advantage. As king of Shoa and later emperor of Ethiopia, he asked representatives from Italy to get him modern weapons, suggested to the French that they build a railroad from the Red Sea to Shoa, and sought a military understanding with the British, who controlled Egypt and the Nile Valley, as well as Kenya to the south and British Somaliland to the east. By making the Europeans compete against each other to gain favor at his court, Menelik got what he wanted and kept any one power from dominating Ethiopia.

ITALY'S EMPIRE IN AFRICA

Latecomers to the game of empire, the Italians emerged as the European power of most concern to Menelik. "The Italians have not come to these parts because they lack . . . abundance in their own country," Menelik warned, " . . . they come . . . to aggrandize themselves."[8] He was right. Building a colonial empire was part of Italy's dream to become a world power. Italy hoped to make Ethiopia's cool and fertile highlands the destination for impoverished Italian peasants. Few of them dared to brave the 120-degree heat in Italy's lowland colonies of Eritrea and Somaliland. Not all Italians favored the push into Ethiopia, but those who did dreamed of a new Roman Empire in East Africa. Britain gave its blessing to Italy's imperial dream, preferring to have weak Italy rather than strong France colonizing the Red Sea region.

As king of Shoa, Menelik not only came to terms with the Italians but even found them useful. In 1879, he signed a treaty that gave special trading privileges to the Italians in Shoa. Italy's aggressiveness, however, did not sit so well with the rulers of other kingdoms in Ethiopia. In 1887, Italy went to war with Ras Alula, who ruled Tigre on Eritrea's border. Alula's soldiers overwhelmed an outnumbered Italian force at Dogali, killing nearly 500 men. When the news reached Europe, Italians could hardly believe that African soldiers had defeated them. None imagined that Dogali was a glimpse of things to come.

As the world's leading power, Britain tried to calm the broils between Italy and Ethiopia. After the battle at Dogali, Queen Victoria sent a message to John IV, Ethiopia's new emperor, saying, "As regards the Italians, we are sorry that you should have disputes with them. They are a powerful nation, with friendly and good intentions." John politely replied to the queen that his people were fighting the Italians "just as you would fight the Abyssinians if they came into England."[9]

FORTIFYING SHOA

Pressure from Italy convinced Menelik that his kingdom needed to modernize to defend itself against European armies. To that end, Menelik began inviting Europeans to settle in Shoa, of whom the most important was Alfred Ilg, a Swiss engineer. Ilg arrived in 1879, learned Amharic, and stayed on as a counselor to Menelik for almost 30 years. As an engineer Ilg gave Menelik helpful advice on a wide range of projects, including bridges, roads, railways, and weaponry.

Soon after Ilg's arrival, one story has it, Menelik asked the engineer if he could make a pair of shoes with the materials at hand. Ilg dutifully presented the emperor with a pair of European-style leather shoes. Pleased, the king then asked Ilg to make a rifle using only local resources. "What is the use of trying?" the engineer replied. "It would cost far more than a fine European rifle, and would be necessarily crude." The king insisted, and Ilg complied.[10] As the anecdote suggests, Menelik was eager to make his kingdom self-sufficient, modern, and strong, especially in weaponry, but the stark reality of underdevelopment meant that the quickest way to strengthen Shoa, and later Ethiopia, was for Menelik to buy what he needed from Europe rather than attempt to spark an industrial revolution.

In 1883 Menelik married Taytu Betul, a remarkable woman who became his most trusted counselor. Taytu, according to one European visitor, "knows the worth of European culture," yet she deeply mistrusted Europeans. "Why do they come here?" Taytu asked. "To help us unselfishly? No. They all want something."[11] Taytu was always present when Menelik met with foreign visitors, and she conferred with him on the best policies to follow to avoid falling under foreign domination.

Menelik ruled a powerful kingdom but was not yet strong enough to challenge Emperor John. To build his forces, Menelik needed additional lands and revenue. For years he waged a series of brutal campaigns against the largely non-Christian Galla people south and east of Shoa. After conquering a territory, he built fortified villages, called *ketema*, and settled soldiers on the land as farmers and herdsmen. Priests from Ethiopia's Church followed, with forcible conversion to Christianity an integral part of Menelik's policy. Tribute and later taxes from the new lands put money in Menelik's coffers.

In 1887, Menelik founded a new capital city—Addis Ababa—farther south than the historic heartland of Shoa but closer to the newly conquered regions. As a result of Menelik's "southern marches," the Christian, Semitic-speaking people of the North assimilated many

Foreign visitors to Ethiopia described Taytu as Menelik's prime minister. The empress, shown here with her husband, was a strong-willed and intelligent ally in Menelik's lifelong struggle to keep his nation independent.

former Muslims and animists (persons who believe that all things in nature have spirits). By 1889, Menelik had more than doubled both the territory and population of Shoa.

MENELIK BECOMES EMPEROR

Although Menelik worried about the encroaching Italians, he was shrewd enough to use them to gain the imperial throne. Having fought and lost against Emperor John at Dogali, Italy looked on Menelik as a progressive who was more open to European influence. When John died in 1889, Menelik seized the moment to declare himself Ethiopia's emperor. Italy approved. One of his first acts was to sign a treaty of friendship that granted Italy special trading privileges in Ethiopia. Many Europeans assumed that Italy's dream of establishing an empire in Ethiopia was at last being realized.

That, however, was not to be. A classic diplomatic conflict unfolded. Article 17 of the treaty stipulated, in Italian, that Ethiopia would *servirsi*, or make use of, Italy's government in all its dealings with foreign powers. To Rome, this meant that Menelik had given up control of his country's foreign policy, making Ethiopia a protectorate of Italy. The Amharic translation of the treaty, however, which was equally valid, stated only that Menelik could communicate with the "Kings of Europe" through Italy. Menelik believed he was under no obligation to do so and that his nation remained a fully sovereign state.

American and European newspapers reported the Italian, not the Amharic, version of the treaty. "The treaty struck with King Menelek practically establishes an Italian protectorate over Abyssinia," the *New York Times* enthused, and thus "opens a new era of civilization to a great part of mysterious Africa."[12] The Italians moved quickly to seize the new power that they read into the treaty. When rebellion flared in several Ethiopian towns bordering their colony in Eritrea, Italian soldiers moved in, allegedly to restore order, but clearly intending to stay.

Menelik continued to believe that he had signed only a treaty of friendship and trade. Taytu reminded him that Emperor John had fought the Italians and asked, "And you, after such an example, want to sell your country?"[13] When Queen Victoria praised Menelik for accepting Italy's protectorate, the emperor fired off a message to Rome declaring that "the contents written in Amharic and the translation in Italian do not conform." Menelik urged Italy to "announce this mistake to the friendly powers" and disavow their claim to a protectorate. In the diplomatic squabble that ensued, Empress Taytu declared, "I am a woman and I do not love war; but rather than accepting this I prefer war."[14] Even a 2 million lira loan from Italy to Ethiopia failed to persuade Menelik that he was Rome's lapdog.

After several years of patient negotiations, Menelik at last rejected the treaty entirely. "Pretending friendship" the king of Italy "has desired to seize my country," he fumed. "Because God gave the crown and power that I should protect the land of my forefathers, I terminate and nullify this treaty . . . My kingdom is an independent kingdom and I seek no one's protection."[15]

IMPERIAL RIVALRIES

In the great game of imperial rivalry, one nation's crisis was another's windfall. Italy's quarrel with Menelik opened the door to France and Russia. The French saw the Italians as nothing more than a surrogate of the British and did all they could to help the emperor, allowing weapons to reach Ethiopia through Djibouti, the French port on the Red Sea. They even ceded Menelik some territory they had long coveted in Somaliland, a French protectorate on Ethiopia's eastern border. Russia and the Ottoman Empire gave Menelik diplomatic support, refusing to recognize Italy's protectorate. Menelik juggled the rival interests, gaining benefits from each without allowing himself to become the tool of any European power.

Less experienced at the imperial game than the other powers, the Italians underestimated the power, organization, and intelligence of the Ethiopians. Most of all they misunderstood how much their own aggressive moves had nourished a new nationalism in Ethiopia, a patriotism that transcended tribe and kingdom. "Menelik is weak, uncertain, and in the hands of his wife," one Italian official noted, "... Public opinion is prepared for the downfall of Menelik. At the first blow the empire will fall to pieces."[16] In fact, building on the unifying work of emperors John and Theodore before him, Menelik had forged a new nation-state in Africa.

From Eritrea, the Italians marched inland. Through telegrams, Prime Minister Francesco Crispi urged General Oreste Baratieri, commander of the Italian forces, to strike a decisive blow against

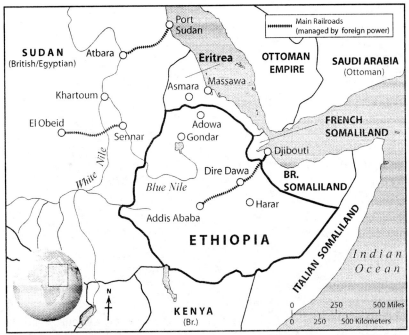

After the Italians took over Eritrea along the Red Sea, Ethiopia was entirely surrounded by colonies and protectorates of Britain, France, and Italy.

Menelik. Italy had opted for conquest, not diplomacy. "Little prospect of peace in Abyssinia," the *New York Times* noted in January 1896. The Italians "will have to fight."[17]

As the moment of truth loomed, Menelik called his people to arms. "Hitherto God has graciously preserved our native land," the emperor declared.

> He has permitted us to conquer our enemies and to reconstitute our Ethiopia. It is by the grace of God that I have reigned hitherto, and if my death is near, I have no anxiety on that account, for death is the fate of all men. But to this day God has never humiliated me. . . .
>
> An enemy is come across the sea. . . . I allowed him to seize my possessions, and I entered into lengthy negotiations with him, in the hope of obtaining justice without bloodshed, but the enemy refuses to listen. He continues to advance, he undermines our territories and our people like a mole. Enough! With the help of God I will defend the inheritance of my forefathers and drive back the invader by force of arms. Let every man who has sufficient strength accompany me. And he who has not, let him pray for us.[18]

THE BATTLE OF ADOWA

Baratieri had amassed an army of some 10,000 Italians and about 8,000 Eritreans for a showdown near the highland village of Adowa. Menelik carefully concealed the size of his own forces, and Baratieri underestimated their number, the quality of their weapons, and their commitment to Ethiopia's independence. Men, women, and children worked through the night to prepare for the battle, building fortifications, filling water jugs, and preparing beds for the wounded. Taytu herself "went with the emperor to the outer limits of the camp and organized the defense perimeter with 5,000 men of her personal army."[19]

Before dawn on Sunday, February 29, Baratieri ordered his troops forward. Menelik and Taytu were at morning prayers when messengers sounded the alarm. The emperor received the sacrament, and then moved swiftly to lead his army. Baratieri did not realize he faced an Ethiopian force of between 80,000 and 100,000 troops.

The armies met at dawn, and before 9 o'clock Italy's catastrophe was clear. By noon Baratieri had sounded the retreat, but it was too late. Armed with rifles and machine guns, the Ethiopians mowed down the fleeing soldiers. Taytu commanded troops alongside her husband, "her cannoneers to the right of where she stood fired so continuously that they succeeded in breaking the center of the enemy army," according to one account.[20] In the end, more than 4,000 Italians died—an astonishing battlefield mortality rate—and nearly 2,000 were captured. Ethiopian losses were about the same, but did not seriously weaken Menelik's much larger force.

The victory at Adowa was one of the great upsets in the history of European empire. Rarely did "natives" win battles against European armies, even with the advantage of greater numbers. Since control of the colonies depended on keeping the local people overawed, it was dangerous for Africans and Asians to discover that they could beat European soldiers. "By this defeat," the London *Times* fretted, "the prestige of European arms as a whole is considerably impaired."[21]

For Italy, the defeat at Adowa was a "disaster" and a "fiasco" that left Italians "awe-struck," as U.S. newspapers put it. In the days following the battle, riots broke out across Italy. Some protested the government's incompetence, while others denounced the whole project of colonizing Ethiopia. In Pisa, students stoned the police and blocked trains carrying soldiers who were shipping out for Africa. Meanwhile, socialists and others who opposed imperialism chanted, "Long live Menelik!"[22] One Italian teenager, Benito Mussolini, burned with shame at his country's defeat at the hands of an African army and vowed to avenge the humiliation.

While Europeans were horrified at the rout of an Italian army by Menelik's troops, Ethiopians celebrated the Battle of Adowa, pictured here, as the victory that saved their country's independence. (*Bridgeman Art Library International*)

SUDDENLY "CIVILIZED"

The Adowa victory remade Ethiopia's reputation on the world stage. The late 1800s was the age of "scientific" racism in Europe and the United States. The best scientists of the time assumed a strict hierarchy of races with Anglo-Saxons on top, Mediterraneans and Slavs in the middle, and Asians and Africans at the bottom. Menelik's victory exploded like an artillery shell among the disciples of racial "science." How could an inferior race defeat a European army?

Within weeks of Adowa, U.S. newspapers were redefining Ethiopians in keeping with the best "science" of the day. Calling Ethiopians "the most gifted of Africans," the *New York Times* pointed out that Menelik's people lived in "the Switzerland of Africa." Ethiopians "are not black, but are of Caucasian descent as pure as the Anglo-Saxon." They are "decidedly a superior race to the other peoples of the Dark Continent." Ethiopia was "literally the cradle of culture and of Christianity" and the forefathers of modern-day Ethiopians were "the oldest and greatest people known to history."[23]

Menelik's star naturally rose after Adowa. Although some Europeans had styled him "a barbarian," he was in fact "very much a gentleman of lofty lineage." Thanks to Menelik's leadership, Ethiopia "is rapidly rising on the road to progress and civilization." The London *Times* noted that the Ethiopians "were a civilized power both in the way they made war and in the way they conducted their diplomacy." The emperor's fame had spread so far by 1898 that a thoroughbred horse named King Menelik ran at New York's Aqueduct racetrack.[24]

Racism persisted, of course, despite Adowa. Still, the fact that one decisive military victory had elevated Ethiopia from barbarism to the cradle of Christianity suggests that civilization, in the eyes of the West, had more to do with raw power than democracy or industrial development. Like the Japanese after their defeat of China in 1895, Ethiopians discovered that nothing impressed the West more than military prowess.

REPERCUSSIONS OF ADOWA

The victory at Adowa had concrete results as well. Within days of the battle, Italy sued for peace. In defeat, Italy gave up its claim to a protectorate and recognized "absolutely and without reserve the independence of the Ethiopian Empire."[25] Menelik was a generous winner, returning the captured Italian soldiers and allowing Italy to keep Eritrea, the colony used as a base for the assault on Ethiopia. The emperor understood that if he launched an all-out war against the Italians, it was likely that Britain would intervene. Even in the euphoria of victory, he had a clear sense of what he could and could not do.

Menelik's handling of the peace negotiations was masterful, and Europeans saw that the Ethiopian victory was not a flash in the pan. Britain, France, Russia, and Germany all revised their views of Menelik and his people, recognizing the country's independence and sending diplomats to meet with the Negus Negasti. In 1897 Britain signed an agreement that ceded thousands of square miles to Menelik, and other treaties clarified Ethiopia's frontiers with the European colonies that surrounded it. Menelik had not only saved his nation's independence—he had also won equal treatment by the Great Powers of Europe, an unparalleled feat for an African leader.

The victory over Italy galvanized Ethiopian national identity, leading some Ethiopians to ridicule European power. A few even objected to Menelik's willingness to compromise with the Europeans. "You started . . . making friends with these white foreigners," one nationalist intellectual wrote to Menelik in 1899. "It is You who let them enter and occupy our country"[26] Realizing that nationalist feeling had never been stronger, Menelik seized the moment to hammer Ethiopia's far-flung kingdoms into a single nation.

FORGING A CENTRALIZED STATE

Like Porfirio Díaz in Mexico, Menelik took steps to strengthen the central government at the expense of provincial rulers. He developed a modern tax system that put his government's finances on a firm footing. "The taxes imposed on the newly incorporated regions," Harold Marcus writes, "not only supported the state, but also forced a more or less unitary economy within the empire."[27] Menelik also centralized the court system. Appeals now went to judges appointed by the emperor instead of by provincial officials.

Again like Díaz, Menelik cracked down on bandits and criminals with merciless, usually capital, punishments. When an American from St. Louis visited Ethiopia in 1904, she noted that the country was "more safe and less difficult to travelers than are some of the New York streets."[28]

Modernization in Ethiopia, as in Mexico, had little to do with democracy. The country had nothing like a congress or parliament. The authority of the emperor had traditionally been limited only by the power of the regional lords, the rases, who had once been kings in their own right. After Adowa, however, Menelik reduced their power, demanding that the rases pledge loyalty to the central government— that is, to him. He also kept modern weapons out of the hands of provincial officials. As a result, regional rebellions became rare. As Robert Skinner, the American diplomat who visited in 1903, put it, "Some of the provincial Princes ruling over great tribes are, to this day, referred to as Kings, but the word no longer has its old meaning . . . for they are merely governors, who derive their authority from Menelik, not merely acknowledging his over lordship, but administering his laws and gathering his taxes."[29]

Although the process of centralization was at times brutal, Menelik expanded Ethiopia's borders to their modern limits and created a far more unified national state. Because of him, Ethiopia was the only nation in Africa to make its own borders rather than having them drawn by European colonizers.

S. M. MENELICK II, Roi des Rois d'Abyssinie

This French postcard, an early example of a souvenir, suggests the fascination that Menelik held for Europeans. The text identifies Menelik as Abyssinia's "roi des rois," or king of kings, the French translation of his Amharic title "Negus Negasti."

ECONOMIC CHANGE

Menelik cared more about power than economic growth per se, yet to some degree political and economic modernization went hand in hand. Addis Ababa grew quickly into the country's business center, as well as its seat of government, and Menelik made the capital a showcase for new technologies. Modern buildings and bridges first appeared there, and a good road connected Addis Ababa to nearby towns. "Nearly everything modern started in the capital," one urban historian notes, including telegraphs, telephones, water-powered cotton mills, movie theaters, and munitions factories.[30]

Menelik sought other ways to modernize the country and in the process win greater respect from the European powers. He built the country's first schools and hospitals and opened a government printing office. He also petitioned the International Postal Union in Switzerland to accept Ethiopia as a member, regular mail delivery being a sign of "civilization." Italy blocked Menelik's initial efforts, however, and Ethiopia was not allowed to join the union until 1908.

Again like Porfirio Díaz, Menelik changed the laws governing landownership, rewarding soldiers by giving them land in newly conquered areas. With those grants, Menelik did away with traditional laws that made the emperor, at least nominally, the owner of all real estate in the nation. The soldier-settlers thus enjoyed the right not only to work the land but to rent or sell it as they saw fit.[31] Later, Menelik made the policy more general through a new inheritance law that allowed land to be passed down from one generation to the next, rather than automatically reverting to the emperor—reforms that established the legal basis of private property.

In another step toward a market-oriented, capitalist economy, Menelik promoted the use of cash rather than barter for the exchange of goods. Starting in the 1890s, he imported coins struck in France and later began to mint coins in Addis Ababa. Circulation of the new "Menelik dollars" also reinforced Ethiopia's growing sense of national identity.

Ethiopia's commerce likewise expanded, although slowly, with Menelik playing a leading role by lending money to Ethiopians and foreigners alike and investing his own wealth in new ventures. An Italian residing in the capital called the emperor *il solo e vero commerciante in Etiopia* (the only true businessman in

Ethiopia).[32] The *New York Times* complimented the emperor's "business acumen" and reported on his investments in the United States.[33] Trade between northern Ethiopia and the newly conquered south passed through Addis Ababa, where Menelik himself inspected exports, including coffee, natural rubber, and leather. As Menelik extended the rule of Christian Abyssinians over conquered regions, the once-dominant Muslim traders lost their grip on commerce, and consequently French, Indian, Greek, and Armenian merchants moved to Addis Ababa, where many of them received concessions from the emperor.

MENELIK'S CONCESSIONS

Concessions were a major instrument of investment throughout the periphery. (You read about Mexico's not-very-successful concession policy in the previous chapter.) Less-developed countries often granted concessions to attract foreign capital to projects like railroads, telephone systems, and factories. Since concessions were contracts granted by the government itself, they promised greater security to investors.

The concessions Menelik gave out often conveyed monopoly rights to producers of goods such as gold, ivory, sugar, wax, soap, salt, and coffee. Since concession holders didn't face any competition, they could expect to earn handsome profits—profits Menelik believed were necessary to get new industries started in his country.

After the Battle of Adowa, Menelik granted two crucial concessions—one for a railroad from the Red Sea to Addis Ababa, and another for the country's first bank, the Bank of Abyssinia. Menelik thought a national bank was "a prerequisite of modern development" and that the railroad was no less vital to economic growth.[34] A French company received the rail concession, while British capitalists held a majority stake in the bank. It was no accident that Menelik granted the two most important concessions to representatives of rival empires. As always, he took care to balance the influence of the different European nations vying to control Ethiopia.

The railroad took many years to build and presented more than the usual financial and engineering challenges. Since Ethiopia had no seacoast, the railroad would have to have its terminus in either French or Italian territory on the Red Sea. Before the Italian defeat at Adowa, Menelik hesitated to throw in with the French. After the battle, he approved a line originating at the French port of Djibouti, climbing into the highlands through Harrar and ending at Addis Ababa. Although a French company was building the line, British investors quickly came to dominate the enterprise. A stand-off between the company and investors halted the work. "The question of the Abyssinian Railway," a newspaper reported in 1902, " . . . remains hopelessly political, involving continued rivalry between France and Great Britain at Menelik's court."[35] In 1906, Britain, France, and Italy finally came to a tripartite agreement that settled their differences in Ethiopia, allowing work on the line to begin again.

The railway advanced slowly, in part because Menelik worried about the economic upheaval that a rail link to the coast might bring. Empress Taytu also understood that a fast and cheap connection to the outer world would expose her subjects to new products, threatening to turn them from self-sufficient producers into consumers of European imports. "Where will our poor country find the resources to satisfy the needs you create?" she asked the railroad promoters. "Do you think our people will be happier than they are now?"[36]

The image on the front cover, also reproduced as a document at the end of this chapter, is from an actual stock certificate of the Ethiopian railroad. The idealized scene envisions the same commercial transformation that Taytu predicted for Ethiopia, but with optimism rather than anxiety. In fact, the railroad did spur "the exploitation of the country's bulk produce as cash crops," but its impact lay in the future.[37] The railway did not reach Addis Ababa until 1917, four years after Menelik's death.

Like the railroad, the Bank of Abyssinia aimed to stimulate trade and exports. The concession, which Menelik granted in 1905, lavished privileges on the bank. The emperor agreed to deposit all the government's tax revenue in the bank, gave it the exclusive right to issue the nation's currency, and prohibited the founding of any other banks in Ethiopia. These generous terms reflected how difficult it was for countries in the periphery to attract foreign capital without granting special privileges in return. The bank was modestly successful in encouraging "all solid and legitimate business, the growth of which naturally results to its own profit."[38]

The concessions, big and small, granted by Menelik were double-edged. They did allow Ethiopia to attract capital and technology from abroad, but as monopolies even the less important concessions limited competition and probably raised prices for consumers. Merchants in Ethiopia protested against them, and Menelik eliminated some concessions toward the end of his reign.

To European governments, Menelik's concessions were more about geopolitics than making money. Concessions for banks and railroads allowed foreigners to control key sectors of a peripheral nation's economy. If concessions were a "tool for economic development by undeveloped states," they were also "a political tool employed by European nations to perpetuate their imperialist agendas."[39] It is testimony to Menelik's skill in diplomacy that even as British and French nationals took key concessions, their governments did not exert undue influence over the emperor or his nation.

Menelik was far more cautious about forcing economic change upon his people than was Porfirio Díaz. He knew that wealthy landowners and Christian priests opposed economic modernization and the foreign influence that accompanied it. Landed gentry feared that economic growth would make agriculture less important and so undercut their power. The clergy worried that a more modern lifestyle would cut Ethiopians off from their traditions, reducing the importance of religion.

Menelik was well aware of these concerns. When a French visitor first demonstrated a telephone to Menelik's court, a group of priests exclaimed, "That machine is inhabited by a demon!" The emperor supposedly quipped that "these priests are cretins," yet he took their fears seriously,[40] and the country's industries remained few and small scale. (See the U.S. government report on Ethiopia's economy at the end of this chapter.)

For Menelik, technology mattered insofar as it helped him to govern Ethiopia. For that reason, he found the telephone to be the most useful of all the imported innovations. By the early 1900s telephone lines connected all the country's main cities, and the emperor used that network to monitor governors in distant parts of the empire, speaking with them almost daily. Where rebellion brewed, Menelik quickly phoned orders to his military staff.

CONCLUSION

In 1907 and again in 1908, Menelik suffered strokes from which he never fully recovered. In 1910 his grandson, Lij Iyasu, became emperor, although for a time Taytu remained the power behind the throne. After years of decline and near paralysis, Menelik died in December 1913. A period of uncertainly followed, but Ethiopia remained unified and, for another generation, independent.

This chapter has highlighted similarities between Menelik and Porfirio Díaz, but the differences between the two are equally striking. As modernizers, the leaders faced very different challenges. Díaz strove to overcome political anarchy in Mexico, and then concentrated on economic development. Menelik faced an assault on his country's independence by European imperialism. That imminent threat made national unity and military power the key goals of his reign. Menelik succeeded in welding many smaller kingdoms into a unified country, what we now refer to as nation-building. Ironically, Italy's inept imperial project in East Africa helped Menelik construct the nation, giving Ethiopians a sense of themselves as one people, united against foreign invaders.

Although he accomplished a great deal, Menelik did not transform his country's economy as Porfirio Díaz did in Mexico. Unlike Japan under the Meiji reformers, Ethiopia "would not undergo the social revolution required to attain security through industrial modernization."[41] As late as 1918, the country's economy was largely premodern, based on subsistence farming, herding, and barter. To some historians, Menelik's caution in the economic sphere denies him the title "modernizer." Yet his political achievements were remarkable. With the exception of Liberia, Ethiopia was the only nation in sub-Saharan Africa to avoid takeover by Europeans, making it "without peers in modern African history."[42]

For people of color all around the world, Menelik's ability to defeat European armies was an inspiration. Intellectuals from the Caribbean and elsewhere in Africa traveled to Addis Ababa to meet the emperor in person. One of Menelik's successors, Ras Tafari, would take the throne as Emperor Haile Selassie. West Indian nationalists looked on Selassie as a messianic figure, the focal point and origin of the religion known as Rastafarianism.

Menelik's reign had other global impacts. As you read, the teenage Benito Mussolini swore to avenge Menelik's victory at

Adowa. Forty years after the battle, as the Fascist leader of Italy, he did just that. Mussolini's assault on Ethiopia in 1936 and the failure of the League of Nations to take strong measures against that aggression were steps toward World War II. At the same time, the fall of one of Africa's few independent states stimulated intellectuals and national- ists across Asia, Latin America, Africa, and the Middle East to push for the liberation of the Third World. That movement was a prelude to the tidal wave of decolonization that swept the periphery after World War II.

SOURCES

■ Menelik Writes to the King of Italy

Soon after he became emperor of Ethiopia in 1889, Menelik II signed a treaty of friendship with Italy. It quickly became clear, however, that Italy had designs on Ethiopia, which bordered its colony in Eritrea. This letter from Menelik to King Umberto of Italy reflects the Ethiopian ruler's concern about Italy's aggressive behavior.

As you read, note the language and tone of the letter. Does Menelik seem familiar with the etiquette of European diplomacy? Explain. Why do you think Menelik mentions Christianity? What does Menelik say about the landlords and bigwigs of Tigré? Why might he have made this point to Umberto?

Antotto, 24 August 1890

I am very happy that your illustrious representative, Count Salimbeni, has arrived safely. Through him we have received your letter, as well as those of the Queen of England and the Emperor of Germany. Majesty, you are aware of the friendship and good rapport that united me with your late, esteemed father. . . . .

Your Majesty is also aware that, at the time your disagreement with then-emperor John began. . . . I was ready to make the treaty you sought with me . . . without knowing that all of Ethiopia would be united under my rule. When definite word of John's death reached me, I told myself that it was my duty to please Italy and my friend King Umberto. . . . I decided to send my brother, ras Maconnen,[43] along with Count Antonelli, in the hope that you would be very pleased and that our friendship would be strengthened. . . .

When I sent ras Maconnen with Count Antonelli it was with the hope that the treaty . . . would be finalized in exactly the form that had been sent to you . . . When, later, ras Maconnen returned and I saw that he had another supplementary treaty, out of friendship with you I accepted many new articles that are not advantageous to our country. . . .

When . . . I asked Count Antonelli, "What does His Majesty desire?" The count . . . replied to me that all you desired was a location with a cooler climate for the soldiers from Massoua,[44] to be used as a refuge

---

Source: From Carlo Zaghi, ed., *Crispi e Menelich nel diario inedito del conte Augusto Salimbeni* (Turin: Industria libraria tipografica editrice, 1956), translated by Cyrus Veeser.

during the hottest months, and nothing more. Then, as Your Majesty knows, at the time that the Treaty of Outchali was concluded in 1889,[45] I gave up the territories indicated in article 3 . . .

When I gave those territories to Italy, it was with the goal of achieving peace and well-being, to avoid war, and to bring civilization into my country, so that my subjects, like yours, through trade, through the sciences, through labor, and so on, could live happily and in harmony, never thinking that you had asked me for a little in order to get much more later. . . .

When Count Antonelli said to me, "Let's decide the question of the borders," and asked that they be fixed beyond Mareb,[46] I replied to him: "If I am called the king of kings of Ethiopia it is because I added Tigré to my realm, and if then you take up to Mareb, what remains to me?". . . . The bigwigs of Ethiopia and large landowners of Tigré have said to me: "How can you let them take our country from us, which we have preserved with our blood in our battles against the Muslims?" I called together all these worthies to consult with them in order not to have a falling out with Italy, and I told them that it is better to have Christians as neighbors than Muslims, and that peace is better than war, so let's give them as far as Chéket in order to avoid bloodshed. And so, despite their complaints, I have given you up to Chéket. . . .

Why have I decided to write to you? It is because previously, for lack of good men, Ethiopia and Italy, being friends, had a falling out and came to bloodshed. Now I don't believe at all that Your Majesty for a morsel of land would go back on your word, given in article 1 of the Treaty of Outchali. . . .

The drawing of the borders is the key to all our business and the proof of the strength of our friendship, and I await impatiently the quick resolution of the border question. . . .

I pray God to give you a long and happy life and for the peace and friendship of our people.

[signed, Menelik II]

Ethiopia from a British Diplomat's Perspective

Augustus Wylde was a British diplomat who spent many years in Ethiopia. In 1901 he published the book *Modern Abyssinia* because, as he said, the attention "of the whole English-speaking race, as well as most of the continental Powers, has been so repeatedly drawn during the last few years to Abyssinia and its present ruler King Menelek."

As you read, ask yourself how Wylde viewed the nation's merchants and what assumptions about "progress" that view reflected. To what factors did he ascribe the victory at Adowa? What did he think of Ethiopians in general, and what did see as their country's future? What statements suggest that Wylde worried about keeping up the prestige that Europeans enjoyed in Africa?

The merchant . . . has had, and has now, more to do with the opening up of Abyssinia than anyone else, and wherever the merchant trades along the main and country roads of the kingdom, there will be found a welcome to the stranger who visits the country with a peaceful intent, as the merchant from whom the countryman gets the most of his news of the outside world, has told him that the foreigner does no harm in his country and welcomes and protects the traveler and stranger. . . .

Abyssinian merchants. . . . can find an immediate market for their produce from the Europeans settled on the coast; and if they consider the price offered a bad one, they have only to wait a few days for a steamer to Egypt, Aden or India, where they get a better price . . . This trade is not confined to the men alone, as there are a good many females who take up trading as a business and own numbers of houses and a good deal of land in Abyssinia. . . .

From my many years' experience of all classes of Abyssinians, very few of them have any wish further than to lead a quiet life and to be left alone . . . accepting a higher state of civilization that years of peace and contact with the outer world can only give them; the chief reason hitherto of their dislike to foreigners has been caused by the priests, who have had ample justification to regard all strangers with suspicion, as they have mostly been missionaries who have tried to alter the religion of the country. . . .

The battle of Adowa . . . solidified the Abyssinian kingdom, and placed King Menelek firmly on the throne. . . . The battle was at first an artillery duel, the Italians doing great havoc with their mountain guns on the dense masses of Abyssinians . . . The Abyssinian quick-firing Hotchkiss guns soon arrived and took up a position on one of the lower slopes of Garima,[47] from which point they were enabled to pour a plunging fire on the Italians. . . . Thus at eleven o'clock, after expending all their artillery and nearly all their small-arm ammunition, and fighting for nearly five hours, the remnants of the left wing of the Italian force surrendered to the Abyssinian king. The Abyssinian troops in this part of the field were now at liberty to be employed helping their compatriots. . . . So ended the day's fight,

---

Source: From Augustus B. Wylde, *Modern Abyssinia* (London: Methuen, 1901).

which was spread over a very large area of country, all favouring the tactics of the defenders of their country and ending so disastrously for Italy. . . .

The Abyssinians acknowledge that they won the victory very cheaply . . . From their spies they knew all about the Italian force and its movements, whereas the Italians knew but little of their enemy's, and General Baratieri[48] had a very bad name at Adowa, owing to the cruelties that took place when he first occupied the town of Adowa, and no one was likely to volunteer him any valuable information. . . . I never heard from the Abyssinians, from the leading men down to the private soldier, one word of disparagement offered against the Italians . . . on the contrary they were all loud in their praise in fighting so bravely. . . .

The Abyssinians, with the exception of the soldiery, as a rule are most polite and will always give way for a European, many of them in the north go so far as to dismount from their animals and make a low bow when one passes. Some of the soldiery, since the defeat of the Italians at Adowa, are most insulting and monopolise the whole of the high road, and try to ride one off when there is plenty of room for all. I always try and get to the side of the road when soldiers pass, so as not to run the risk of being insulted, but I am afraid European prestige in some places in the country is on the wane.

Ethiopia's Economy through American Eyes

By the early 20th century, American companies were aggressively seeking out markets around the world with the help of U.S. officials. The United States signed a trade agreement with Menelik in 1903, and the official report excerpted below informed Americans of business opportunities in Ethiopia. Written just five years after Menelik's death, the report gives a view of Ethiopia's economy from a decidedly American perspective.

Compare this document with Wylde's assessment of Ethiopia. Were the authors in basic agreement or not? Explain. Does the snapshot of Ethiopia's economy correlate with the description of premodern societies in the introduction to this book? In what ways does the report reflect the racial thinking of the early 20th century?

Introduction

The commercial status of Abyssinia has in the last few years been of increasing interest to the leading trading nations of the world. . . .

Abyssinia Backward in Economic Development

Abyssinia has been backward in economic development, owing mainly to its former almost complete isolation and inaccessibility; to the almost total lack of adequate transportation facilities, banks, and other similar aids to trade; to the apparent disinclination of the Government to encourage foreign trade; and to the consequent lack of business stability and confidence. There is a noticeable improvement in these conditions, but trade development is still in its infancy.

The present purchasing power of the Abyssinians is undoubtedly small, but it is not limited except by the desires of the people. The country is rich, so that, as their desire for foreign manufactured goods is educated and increased, they have only to plant larger crops and raise more animals to secure an increase in their supply of dollars and incidentally in the average purchasing power. This is now happening. . . .

Extent of the Market

. . . .As may be expected in a country so wealthy in natural resources, with a comparatively good climate and populated by 8,000,000 to 10,000,000 of intelligent and aggressive people, the commercial future is rich and full of promise. . . . While the Abyssinians have not yet taken to trade in any considerable numbers, the few merchants of that race who have been observed are keen and intelligent traders. . . .

Special Conditions Governing Trade

Trade in Abyssinia is often very much a matter of barter or indirect exchange of imported goods for Abyssinian products. . . . The principal products of Abyssinia, such as hides, skins, coffee, wax, ivory, and civet,[49] all have a ready market. . . .

Character of Population

. . . . The average Abyssinian is a proud, aggressive, and fairly intelligent individual. He is not progressive and has shown a decided disinclination to open his country to modern economic and social progress. He has been suspicious of all advances made by foreigners, and that is the principal

---

Source: From U.S. Bureau of Foreign and Domestic Commerce, *Abyssinia: Present Commercial Status of the Country with Special Reference to the Possibilities for American Trade* (Washington: Government Printing Office, 1918).

reason why his rich country is still so little known commercially. This condition seems, however, to be improving gradually. . . .

Primitive Agricultural Methods

In general, Abyssinia is said to be unequaled by any other part of Africa as an agricultural country. The people have always lived principally on the results of agriculture, and the rich soil and favorable climate have made it possible for them to live comparatively well. The agricultural methods are primitive. . . .

Mining Industry Undeveloped

The mining industry in Abyssinia is undeveloped. There are many reported evidences of commercial deposits of coal, iron, oil, sulphur, gold, silver, copper, and potash. . . . The coal is undoubtedly good and present in commercial quantities, but immediate development of the deposits in unlikely on account of their inaccessibility. . . .

No Important Manufacturing Industries

There are no important manufacturing industries in Abyssinia. Manufacturing is confined principally to a few sawmills near Adis Abeba,[50] two or three flour mills with limited output, small soap-making establishments, and small tanneries. . . .

Home Industries

The Abyssinians have a number of home industries, the principal ones being the weaving of native garments of wool and cotton cloth; the making of mats and baskets; and crude gold, silver, and iron working. The products of all these home industries are consumed locally. The weaving of cotton cloth is the only one of interest to foreign trade. . . .

Market for Manufactured Goods

The principal requirements for manufactured goods . . . are confined mainly to cotton fabrics and yarns; iron and steel bars, corrugated-iron roofing, enamelware, and hardware in general; wines and liquors; soap and scent; silks and silk thread; felt hats; and sewing machines. . . .

Conclusion

The Abyssinian market is an undeveloped one with great future possibilities. While the actual purchasing power of the people is quite limited, their potential purchasing power is important. Their demands have heretofore been confined to such actual necessities as food and clothing. Their food has mostly been produced within the country, as has a small part of their clothing. As trade routes have been opened up they have come to know and appreciate foreign manufactured cotton fabrics. . . . and as the demand is very plainly growing, there is no doubt as to the value of the market.

■ Ethiopian Railroad Stock Certificate

This image of Menelik II adorns an Ethiopian railroad stock certificate issued in Paris in 1899. Since the success of the project depended on the willingness of Europeans to invest in Africa, the railroad promoters naturally showed Menelik's Ethiopia in the most positive light imaginable. How does the image suggest Menelik's religion, his military prowess, his devotion to modernity, and his country's potential as a trading partner?

NOTES

1. Robert P. Skinner, *Abyssinia of To-Day* (New York: Negro Universities Press, 1969), pp. 86–87.

2. Quoted in Harold G. Marcus, *Life and Times of Menelik II: Ethiopia 1844–1913* (London: Oxford University Press, 1975), p. 11.

3. Ibid., p. 23.

4. Ibid., pp. 43–44.

5. Ibid., p. 47.

6. Herbert Vivian, *Abyssinia: Through the Lion-Land to the Court of the Lion of Judah* (New York: Negro Universities Press, 1969), p. 201.

7. "The Emperor Menelik," *Times* (London), June 15, 1897, p. 7.

8. Quoted in Sven Rubenson, *The Survival of Ethiopian Independence* (London: Heinemann, 1976), p. 380.

9. Quoted in Marcus, *Life and Times*, pp. 97–98.

10. Skinner, *Abyssinia of To-Day*, p. 98.

11. Chris Prouty, *Empress Taytu and Menilek: Ethiopia 1883–1910* (Trenton, NJ: Red Sea Press, 1986), pp. 276–277.

12. "Italy in Abyssinia," *New York Times*, November 19, 1889, p. 4; "Italy in Africa," *New York Times*, December 14, 1889, p. 4.

13. Quoted in Marcus, *Life and Times*, p. 126.

14. Ibid., pp. 127, 130.

15. Quoted in Paul B. Henze, *Layers of Time: A History of Ethiopia* (London: Hurst, 2000), p. 162.

16. Ibid., p. 167.

17. "Italians Will Have to Fight," *New York Times*, January 27, 1896, p. 5.

18. Quoted in Skinner, *Abyssinia of To-Day*, pp. 145–146.

19. Prouty, *Empress Taytu*, p. 156.

20. Ibid.

21. "The Italian Disaster in Abyssinia," *Times* (London), March 4, 1896, p. 5.

22. "Italy is Awe-Struck," *New York Times*, March 5, 1896, p. 1; "Italy's Wrathful Mobs," *New York Times*, March 7, 1896, p. 1; "Italy's African Fiasco," *New York Times*, July 5, 1896, p. 16; "Ministry May Resign," *Washington Post*, March 4, 1896, p. 2; "Italians Lost Heart," *Washington Post*, March 7, 1896, p. 1.

23. "The Most Gifted of Africans," *New York Times*, April 19, 1896, p. 29; "In Christian Abyssinia," *New York Times*, May 4, 1896, p. 9.

24. "Menelik and His Empire," *New York Times*, September 25, 1998, p. 7; "The Races at Aqueduct," *New York Times*, November 1, 1898, p. 5; *Times* (London) quoted in Paulos Milkias and Getachew Metaferia, eds., *The Battle of Adwa* (New York: Algora, 2005), p. 218.

25. Quoted in Marcus, *Life and Times*, p. 177.

26. Irma Taddia, "Ethiopian Source Material and Colonial Rule in the Nineteenth Century: The Letter to Menelik (1899) by Blatta Gabra Egzi'abeher," *Journal of African History* 35: 3 (1994), pp. 511–512.

27. Marcus, *Life and Times*, pp. 1–2.

28. "Woman Tells of Her Abyssinian Travels," *New York Times*, July 18, 1904, p. 8.

29. Skinner, *Abyssinia of To-Day*, p. 146.

30. Peter P. Garretson, *A History of Addis Ababa* (Wiesbaden: Verlag, 2000), p. 144.

31. Ibid., pp. 13–14.

32. Ibid., p. 106.

33. "Menelik as Business Man," *New York Times*, October 30, 1910, p. C4; "King Menelik Has Investments Here," *New York Times*, November 7, 1909, p. C4.

34. Charles Schaefer, "The Politics of Banking: The Bank of Abyssinia, 1905–1931," *International Journal of African Historical Studies* 25: 2 (1992), p. 362.

35. "The Abyssinian Railway," *New York Times*, February 8, 1902, p. 1.

36. Prouty, *Empress Taytu*, p. 219.

37. Harold Marcus, *A History of Ethiopia* (Berkeley: University of California, 2002), p. 107.

38. United States Bureau of Foreign and Domestic Commerce, *Abyssinia: Present Commercial Status of the Country with Special Reference to the Possibilities for American Trade* (Washington: Government Printing Office, 1918), p. 36.

39. Schaefer, "Politics of Banking," p. 366.

40. Prouty, *Empress Taytu*, p. 237.

41. Marcus, *History of Ethiopia*, p. 106.

42. Teshale Tibebu, *Making of Modern Ethiopia, 1896–1974* (Lawrenceville, NJ: Red Sea, 1995), p. 49.

43. Actually Menelik's first cousin. Ras Maconnen (1852–1906) was an important and loyal administrator, diplomat, and general and the father of Emperor Haile Selassie.

44. A Red Sea port in the Italian colony of Eritrea.

45. A treaty that delineated the border between Ethiopia and the Italian colony of Eritrea.

46. A river in northern Ethiopia, in the region of Tigré, that forms a partial natural border between Ethiopia and Eritrea.

47. Abba Garima, a mountain near Adowa. Italians usually refer to the battle of Adowa as the battle of Abba Garima.

48. General Oreste Baratieri (1841–1901), governor of Eritrea.

49. Musk from the perineal glands of the civet, an Ethiopian mammal, is used in the production of perfume.

50. Menelik II transformed Adis Abeba into Ethiopia's capital in 1889.

Sun Yatsen:
Revolutionary Outsider

Like Mexico and Ethiopia, China could not escape the West's growing wealth and power in the 1800s. Vast and well-organized, China brought advantages to that confrontation that no other non-Western nation could boast. For over 2,000 years, China had been a largely unified state, with one government, a written language, and a stable agrarian economy. Indeed, China had dominated East Asia for centuries—its neighbors, including Japan, Korea, and Vietnam, all paid tribute to China in recognition of that dominance. It was natural for the emperors of China to see their nation as the center of the world, the source of all civilization—the Celestial Empire.

When European ships first arrived in China's coastal cities, the emperor saw them as an annoyance. Even after Britain defeated the emperor's war junks in the Opium War of the early 1840s and Europeans won the right to carve out enclaves in China's port cities, Chinese leaders were slow to grasp the enormous change in world power that was underway. At first, these European zones had little impact on China's internal market or its political system, but eventually the foreigners presented a life-or-death challenge to the empire.

Given the inward gaze of China's rulers, it was no accident that the man who championed China's modernization had lived abroad for many years. Born to a peasant family, Sun Yatsen (1866–1925), as he is known in the West (but known to the Chinese by the honorific Sun Zhongshan), escaped a life working on the land and received an education at a British school in Hawai'i. Banished by China's government as a dangerous rebel, Sun traveled widely, read voraciously, and studied foreign governments up close. Countries that had modernized rapidly, especially the United States and Japan, attracted him the most. "We once thought we could not do what the Europeans could do," Sun declared, "We see now that . . . if we follow Japan, we, too, will be learning from the West as Japan did."[1]

For a man who would be hailed as *Guofu*, the father of his country, Sun was in many ways decidedly un-Chinese: He spoke fluent English, dressed in European suits, and became a devout Christian. Nevertheless, Sun was the uncontested leader of a far-flung revolutionary movement that stretched from China's mainland to Tokyo, London, and New York. His life was often in danger—China offered the princely sum of $180,000 to catch him, dead or alive—yet he made time to write about his vision of China's future. Sun's program for a new China combined ancient elements with the latest Western ideas about government and provided a blueprint for revolutionaries.

In 1911, while Sun was in the United States raising money for the movement, China's 2,000-year-old imperial order finally collapsed. After getting off a train in Denver, Sun opened a newspaper and read that the revolutionaries were calling him home to become China's first president. Sun went back, but served as acting president for only a few months. Unlike Porfirio Díaz and Menelik II, he never held power long enough to direct his nation's future. Yet his vision of a modern China, and the political party he founded, shaped events from 1911 until the victory of Mao Zedong and the Communist Party in 1949.

THE WORLD'S GREATEST PREMODERN STATE

China's encounter with the West was extraordinarily complex because China was the most successful premodern state in world history, having been united into a single empire in 221 BCE. A major factor in China's success was its orderly system of government. Centuries before European states had bureaucracies, China set up ministries with clearly defined duties for taxes, public works, war, personnel, punishment, and ceremonies. Equally important to the empire's stability was a triple-tiered examination system that provided the basis for selecting government officials. To pass the three increasingly difficult examinations, young men spent years studying classic Confucian texts and approved commentaries on them. The exams were so rigorous that most candidates never succeeded in passing all three, and those who did were often in their 30s or older. Only after passing the second examination did these scholars start their careers as government officials. In theory, any Chinese man could sit for the exams, making the system a *meritocracy*. In practice, however, it was mostly the sons of wealthy families who had the resources to prepare for the exams.

The examination system meant that all Chinese officials were masters of the same ancient texts. Thus, they tended to share a worldview that helped unify an empire with provinces as big and as populous as European countries. China has one of the world's oldest written languages, stretching back over 3,000 years, and the empire's past was well documented in thousands of volumes of history. When China faced a crisis, its scholar-officials naturally looked to the past for guidance. No nation's culture can be summed up in a few sentences, yet it is fair to say that the Confucian system absorbed by the scholars emphasized order, hierarchy, and mutual obligations—for example, between a father and his children. Subjects owed loyalty to the emperor, the heavenly mandated father of his people, but the emperor's mandate had limits. Confucianism taught that the masses could rebel against an immoral or unjust leader because "Heaven sees as the people see." In other words, an unjust emperor would lose the Mandate of Heaven, which the Chinese saw as an impersonal, cosmic moral force. The ultimate goal of the complex system was stability, a fitting philosophy for the planet's longest-lived state.

Although the empire was remarkably stable, its history was not without upheavals. From time to time, China suffered conquest by non-Chinese, such as the Mongols in the 1200s and the Manchus in the 1600s. Generally, however, its conquerors adopted China's language and laws and preserved the imperial form of government. The conquerors, in other words, became Chinese. That certainly describes what happened with the Manchus, a semi-nomadic people from a region north of China proper, who created the Qing Dynasty (1644–1911/12). In the words of John King Fairbank, a "thin stratum of Manchu conquerors kept their grip on gargantuan China" by preserving as much of the old system as possible. The Manchus became good Chinese, although China's ethnic majority, the Han, always saw them as outsiders.[2]

BARBARIANS AT THE GATE

The Manchus were securely in power when European ships began to appear regularly in Chinese waters. The country that the Europeans intruded upon was far from static. Long the most densely populated region on earth, China's population had doubled, from 150 to 300 million, during the 1700s. Chinese agriculture was sophisticated, but even so it could not keep up with this demographic surge. More people meant less food, more poverty, and greater discontent. The Taiping Rebellion, really a civil war, raged from 1851 to 1864 and resulted in at least 20 million deaths. Other rebellions erupted as well, leading to a catastrophic decline in population.

To officials focused on internal catastrophes like the Taiping Rebellion, the threat posed by the West must have seemed distant indeed, which helps explain why the encroachment of Europeans did not push China to remake itself, as Japan did after Commodore Perry arrived. More important, the very factors that made China extraordinarily stable also made it extraordinarily hard to change. The Manchus survived the rebellions at mid-century and came to terms with the Europeans. The empire staggered forward, and while it did, few Chinese could imagine what might replace a system that had endured for thousands of years.

China's reverence for the past was not helpful in the changed world after 1800. From time immemorial, China's only real enemies had been nomads who galloped their horses on the steppes north and west of China proper. The Great Wall, really a series of walls built over many centuries, had been constructed to keep these nomads out. Despite coastal attacks by Japanese and Korean pirates, China had never faced a serious threat from the sea. When Europeans arrived in their warships, the emperor did not even have a way to negotiate with the odd-looking foreigners. China had been the only Great Power in the East for so many centuries that the Western concept of diplomacy, meaning peaceful relations among equal states, did not exist. Chinese diplomacy centered on the tributary principle, whereby neighboring peoples, such as the Koreans and Japanese, paid tribute to the emperor in the form of gifts.

Contact with the West produced a revolution in the old ways of thinking. In the 1840s, officials still referred to Europeans as barbarians and dogs. By the 1860s, they stopped calling Europeans *Yi*, or "barbarians," and adopted the more neutral *yang*, "foreigners." Officials also accepted the modern idea that the world was made up of sovereign states with equal rights. Slowly, grudgingly, Chinese officials admitted to themselves that they needed to learn from the West—at least in some areas.

SELF-STRENGTHENING TO SAVE THE EMPIRE

As in other premodern societies suddenly confronted by the West, China's leaders at first assumed that a better army and navy, and better weapons, could neutralize the advantages of the industrialized nations. To defend China from the West, the government created schools to train specialists in foreign languages, as well as experts in military and naval technology, mining, shipbuilding, and telegraph communication. The goal was to preserve the empire and as much of traditional China as possible. Officials called their modernization policy *ziqiang* (self-strengthening) a concept that disguised the need to learn from the West inasmuch as it was derived from the *Yijing*, or *Classic of Changes*, an ancient text composed long before Confucius lived.

Reformers in the government saw Western knowledge as a set of practical skills that could be grafted onto the ancient trunk of Chinese tradition. "Chinese learning as the base," as a famous saying of the time put it, "Western studies for use."[3] In reality, it was difficult to combine the two. In the Introduction we saw that Japan learned about the West by sending students to the United States and Europe. China tried the same strategy—briefly. In the 1870s, some 120 Chinese students arrived at Yale University, where the young men studied hard and even learned to play baseball but did not memorize the Chinese classics. When they returned home, the students could not sit for the civil service exams. Appalled, Chinese officials ended the experiment.

If the imperial government was halting in its embrace of Western knowledge, other Chinese were not. After Britain defeated China in the Opium War (1840–1842), Europeans and Americans won the right to create "international zones" in Chinese port cities. Chinese laws did not apply in these zones—extraterritoriality gave foreigners the right to judge their own citizens. The foreigners proceeded to make the treaty ports into miniature versions of European cities, with broad, paved roads, gas and later electric lighting, and modern wharf and port facilities. Unlike the vast majority of peasants in the interior, Chinese living in coastal cities had direct contact with Westerners. Some treaty-port Chinese worked for Europeans, while others went into business with them. Many admired the technical progress of the West. Yet even those who had good relations with Westerners disliked their arrogance, their ignorance of China's past, and their readiness to intimidate the imperial government. In other words, many Chinese in the treaty ports developed a love–hate relationship with the West.

SUN YATSEN AND THE OVERSEAS CHINESE

Sun Yatsen emerged from this blending of East and West in China's "foreign fringe."[4] He was born in 1866 in the small southern village of Cuiheng, along the Pearl River, not far from the major port city of Guangzhou, which the English and Americans called Canton. Of all China's cities, Guangzhou had the most contact with the West since it was just upriver from both the Portuguese colony at Macao and Hong Kong, a British concession city.

The first of many life-changing events for Sun was his brother Sun Mei's decision to migrate to Hawai'i, at the time an independent kingdom. When Sun was 12 years old, his brother invited him to Hawai'i and sent him to an exclusive British school in Honolulu, where Sun became a fluent English speaker and also encountered American Protestant missionaries. Sun assimilated quickly—too quickly for his brother's taste. When Sun Mei learned that Sun Yatsen planned to be baptized, he angrily sent the boy home to China.

Back in Cuiheng, the 16-year-old Sun saw the small village in a new light—locked in the past and gripped by superstition. Although he had not yet declared himself a Christian, Sun strongly objected to the traditional Chinese practice of paying respect to idols that represented gods. One night, Sun and a friend broke into a village temple and smashed several wooden idols, making him, quite literally, an iconoclast. Humiliated and afraid for Sun's safety, his family agreed that the boy should leave Cuiheng, this time for a school in nearby Hong Kong. There Sun broke with his family's wishes and Chinese tradition by accepting baptism and joining the Congregational Church.

As Sun was finishing his undergraduate work, a professor urged him to enroll at a new British medical college in Hong Kong. The idea of using modern science to cure disease appealed to Sun, who had little faith in traditional remedies. Sun stayed on to study medicine, thriving in the climate of friendly contact among educated Chinese and Westerners. Discussions among students and faculty often went beyond science to address the problem of modernizing China under Manchu rule. Sun earned his medical degree in 1892, but did not practice long. Events in the 1890s turned him from curing individuals to saving the nation.

FROM MEDICINE TO POLITICS

In 1893 the young doctor learned that a high government official, Li Hongzhang, was planning to create a national medical school in northern China. Li, one of the main movers of the "self-strengthening" group at the imperial court in Beijing, was known to have a great deal of influence with the Guangxu Emperor (in power 1875–1908), who was in his early 20s. Guangxu ruled in name only. Real power lay in the hands of a woman, Empress Dowager Cixi, a brilliant, ruthless conservative who maneuvered to keep reform minimal. The empress dowager feared that if China modernized, the imperial structure would be replaced by an elected government.

As one of a handful of Chinese doctors trained in Western medicine, Sun hoped Li would make him an instructor at the new college. When Sun traveled to Beijing to see Li, however, his ambitions ran far beyond getting a job. In his pocket he carried a detailed plan to modernize China, calling for dramatic reform not only of medicine but also of public education, agriculture, trade, transportation, and industry. Sun had never sat for even the first of the civil service exams, so it was bold, arrogant even, to presume that one of China's most powerful men would listen to him. In fact, Li Hongzhang refused even to see Sun in Beijing. Disappointed, the young doctor returned to his practice in Guangzhou, where he published his petition to Li, excerpts of which appear with this chapter's sources.

When Li ignored this overture, Sun gave up reforming China from within. He now saw that the first step toward a modernized China was political change. The ancient imperial system had to go, replaced by a republic based on broad popular support. A republic would embrace public education and the development of industry that would bring China to the level of other powerful states. The imperial government would never do so, out of fear that economic change would undermine its power. "Anyone who . . . knows the people by whom the Emperor is surrounded and influenced," Sun declared, "must know that he is powerless for effectively carrying out the drastic reforms necessary."[5]

The acid test of the official policy of self-strengthening came in 1894, when China went to war with Japan. The Chinese had traditionally seen that island nation as an unimportant backwater. But Japan, transformed by 25 years of rapid modernization, won an easy victory over its much larger neighbor. When Li Hongzhang represented China at the peace conference that ended the war in 1895, Japanese officials scoffed at the self-strengthening movement that he had championed. "Why is it," one Japanese negotiator asked, "that up to now not a single thing has been changed or reformed?" Li admitted that "affairs in my country have been so confined by tradition that I could not accomplish what I desired."[6]

FROM REFORMER TO REVOLUTIONARY

Like an earthquake, the Sino-Japanese War alerted educated Chinese to deep structural flaws that threatened their nation. In this charged atmosphere, medicine no longer held Sun's attention. In November 1894, a few months after the start of the war, he helped organize *Xing Zhong Hui*, the innocently named Society to Restore China's Prosperity. Ostensibly set up to promote the economic reforms that Sun had spelled out in his letter to Li Hongzhang, the group in fact assumed that China stood on the verge of destruction. "Affairs in China are going wrong," the founders declared. "The whole nation is confused. Nobody understands. There is nobody to save the situation. How then is calamity to be averted?"[7]

In the war with Japan, calamity was not averted, and Sun decided that the moment for decisive action had come. With a group of trusted friends, he planned a bold attack to capture Guangzhou, believing that after the humiliating defeat by Japan, the Chinese masses would rise up against the emperor, once a first blow was struck. The young radicals knew little about running a conspiracy, however, and officials in Guangzhou found out that they were gathering guns and dynamite. The police arrested over 70 conspirators, executing several, including one of Sun's closest friends. Sun narrowly escaped, but the Chinese government had now identified him as a public enemy. For the next 15 years, Sun would be able to return to China only briefly, using false papers and at the risk of his life.

Unable to organize inside China, Sun made his way to London. There he visited a British doctor, a friend from his time in medical school. Sun had no idea that Chinese officials were about to make him an international celebrity. One afternoon, Sun disappeared. His friends searched frantically for a week but found no trace of him. Then an anonymous message arrived at the doctor's house: "There is a friend of yours imprisoned in the Chinese Legation . . . they intend sending him out to China, where it is certain they will hang him."[8]

The doctor at once alerted the British government, as well as the press, and soon newspaper readers around the world knew of Sun's kidnapping and the efforts of the British government to win his release. Sun remained a captive for 12 days. When Chinese officials at last bowed to British pressure and released him, Sun emerged a hero. Westerners who knew nothing else about China had heard of Sun Yatsen. His London escape naturally made him a legend among overseas Chinese from London to Singapore, a legend that Sun exploited to help raise money for the cause.

Many Chinese from the towns and villages of South China had gone abroad. This *diaspora* had led to the growth of Chinese communities across Southeast Asia, where the immigrants often dominated retail trade and import–export businesses. Some Chinese traveled even farther from home—to Hawai'i, California and New York, Latin America, and Europe. Sun Yatsen would spend the next 15 years circulating among these communities, sleeping in cheap hotels, meeting with supporters in the back rooms of restaurants, endlessly arguing that China must become a republic and always asking for money.

His message found willing listeners among diaspora Chinese, who often faced discrimination and sometimes violence in their host countries. In the United States, for example, rioters killed dozens of Chinese in the 1870s, leading Congress to ban all immigration from China in 1882. Because the Manchu government was too weak to defend the overseas Chinese diplomatically, these communities bankrolled the movement to overthrow the empire and modernize their homeland.

REVOLUTION FROM AFAR

Despite the hardships of exile, Sun never lost hope. China "resembles a forest of dry wood," he insisted. "It needs only one spark . . . to set the whole mass into flames."[9] But who would strike that first spark? Raising money from expatriates would accomplish nothing unless Chinese at home took action. The scholar-officials, China's ruling class, were far too comfortable to risk all in a revolutionary movement. "When I first began to think about revolution," Sun later wrote, " . . . the official upper classes could not be interested."[10] Sun, or rather his supporters inside China, focused instead on recruiting merchants, workers, and peasants, making contact with secret societies, like the Triad, which had many working-class members in rural China. Since local rebellions flared up regularly, the revolutionaries hoped to seize upon issues that mattered to peasants and workers, such as high land rents or rice shortages, and use them to trigger a broader revolt.

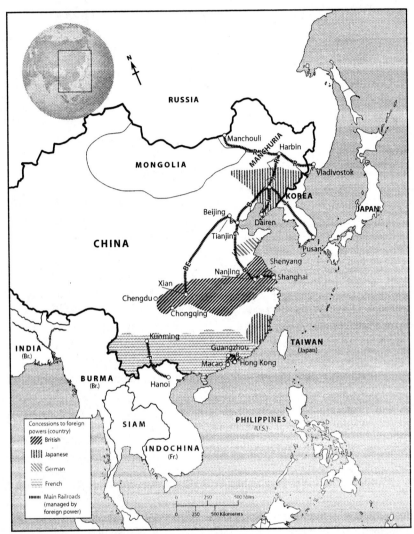

By the early 20th century China's independence had been undermined by the creation of European and Japanese spheres of influence, as shown on the map.

THE BOXERS

Meanwhile, China lurched from crisis to crisis. After Japan's victory over China, Western powers took advantage of the Manchu government's weakness to seize new territory and extract hundreds of new concessions. The emperor himself at last realized that self-strengthening had failed and that China was at risk of being divided up among the Great Powers. In 1898, he allowed Kang Youwei, a leading advocate of change, into the Forbidden City for an audience. "China will soon perish," Kang told the Guangxu Emperor boldly. Soon after, the emperor launched the Hundred Days Reforms, issuing some 40 decrees to modernize schools, the economy, the military, the legal system, and government. The program never went into effect, however, since the empress dowager put the young emperor under house arrest and executed many reformers. Kang escaped to Japan.

Though the empress dowager clung to power, the empire was losing control over its own people. Ordinary Chinese reacted with horror when Japan defeated the Celestial Empire in war, and then watched with shame as their government meekly submitted to Western demands for special privileges. Anger against foreigners, both Westerners and Japanese, boiled below the surface. If the emperor would not protect China, the people themselves would do so. In 1900, the Boxer Rebellion exploded in a wave of attacks on missionaries and Chinese converts to Christianity. When popular support for the Boxers became clear, the empress dowager threw in with the rebels to save herself and the Manchu regime. "China is weak," she observed. "The only thing we can depend upon is the hearts of the people. If we lose them, how can we maintain our country?"[11] As the violence spread across northern China, thousands of foreigners took refuge in Beijing's diplomatic quarter.

Watching from abroad, Sun hoped the Boxer uprising was the start of the revolution he had been waiting for. He and his followers attempted to direct the rage of the people away from foreigners and against the Manchus. Sun's supporters took up arms and fought for control of southern China, and American newspapers reported that "Sun-Yat-Sen aims at deposing the Dowager Empress and making a clean sweep of the existing regime."[12] There were, in fact, two distinct revolutions going on in China: Sun's "rebel forces in the south . . . which are anti-dynastic and friendly to foreigners," the *New York Times* reported, and "the Boxer rebellion in the north, which is pro-dynastic and anti-foreign."[13] In the end, both rebellions failed. Armies loyal to the emperor defeated Sun's forces in the south. In the north, a rescue expedition of European, American, and Japanese troops routed the Boxers and liberated the foreigners, who had been under siege in Beijing for 55 days.

Sun's attempt to channel popular anger against the Manchus had failed, but it revealed an important issue. Although Sun wanted to make China a powerful republic, he had not suffered directly at the hands of foreigners—indeed, quite the opposite. Sun had European,

Japanese, and American friends, many of whom gave money to his movement. Moreover, as a Christian, Sun appreciated the work of the same missionaries who aroused intense hostility on the mainland. He also firmly believed that foreign investment was essential to China's modernization. Yet to most Chinese, the goal of creating a free and prosperous China could not be reached without expelling foreigners, who controlled so much of the economy and seemed bent on destroying Chinese culture. Could a Chinese nationalist *not* be anti-foreign? The problem would return to haunt Sun in later years.

BLUEPRINT FOR A NEW CHINA

In the aftermath of the failed Boxer uprising, Sun reflected on what would replace the 2,000-year old imperial system once the Manchus fell. Democracy? Military dictatorship? Foreign intervention? Sun began to work out some basic principles to guide the revolution he was sure would come. He eventually called his work *Sanmin Zhuyi* (The Three Principles of the People).

Nationalism Sun's first principle, nationalism, assumed that China could survive as a nation only by getting rid of the Qing dynasty. Although the Manchus had ruled China for 250 years, they were foreigners, distinct from the Han ethnic majority. Sun blamed these "foreigners" for corrupting the government and, especially, for closing China off from contact with the West. "When the Manchus seized imperial power . . . the present era of utter misrule began. Then the study of geography, law, history, and science was forbidden," he declared.[14] It was not fair to blame the Manchus for all that was wrong with China, but it made for good propaganda. If the Manchus were the problem, the solution was simple—kick them out. Sun implied that once the Han majority ruled a Chinese republic, many of China's problems would melt away. That, unfortunately, would not prove to be the case.

Democracy The second basic principle, democracy, asserted the right of ordinary Chinese to choose their leaders. In Mexico and Ethiopia, democracy played no part in modernization. China was different. Sun argued that the passive peasant masses had to become active citizens. He knew that the power of the West came in large part from releasing the "boundless creativity" of ordinary people through education and political participation. Since the Chinese people had no experience of self-government, however, Sun favored a three-stage transition to democracy. After the Manchus fell, a military government would keep order and defend against foreign invasion. After three years the military rulers would allow elections under a provisional constitution, and after six more years a fully empowered parliament and president would at last be elected.

Sun's support of democracy was, in part, self-serving. Unlike Porfirio Díaz and Menelik II, Sun was not yet the leader of his country. He was, in fact, a rebel, and to overthrow the Qing dynasty he needed the support of the people. It was also true that Sun was the son of a peasant who had suffered from the snobbery of China's exam-taking elite. "I am a coolie and the son of a coolie," he admitted, using the derogatory word for a Chinese peasant. " . . . My sympathies have always been with the struggling mass."[15] Nevertheless, Sun had traveled a long way from his peasant origins. By 1900 he was an international celebrity, a Western-educated doctor who spoke fluent English and Japanese, as well as Chinese. He had little in common with the illiterate farmers who made up China's vast majority.

It is not surprising, then, that Sun and his followers never had much luck recruiting peasants to their movement. They always had more success with students, military cadets, and other upwardly mobile groups. Sun and his fellow revolutionaries tended to see the illiterate masses primarily as the source of the fighters they needed to overthrow the Manchus. Sun expected peasants to support his policies, not to become political actors in their own right. In keeping with this attitude, Sun recommended that the new republic maintain a version of the old examination system. Requiring government officials to pass a test (a different test, of course, based on modern education, not study of the classics) would, Sun hoped, guarantee that only qualified individuals held office in the new republic. It also meant that the peasant majority would be excluded from office in the new China.

Livelihood Sun's third principle has been translated as *socialism* and also *equalization*, but it was more than either of these. Sun used an ancient Chinese term, *minsheng*, which means the material well-being of the people, what he called *livelihood*. At the time China was still an overwhelmingly agrarian country—more than 80 percent of the people were peasant farmers. To improve the lives of the masses, Sun believed China needed to move away from agriculture toward industrialization.

During his years in Europe and the United States, however, Sun had witnessed the social conflicts that came with industrial growth. "Though Western countries are powerful," he wrote, "their people are really in distress." Workers often went on strike, and Western governments used the police and even the army against strikers. Growing inequality, with millions of low-paid industrial workers and a few fabulously rich capitalists, fueled the growth of socialism and anarchism across Europe. "If the majority of the people fall under the yoke of a few capitalists—is this civilization or is it barbarism?" Sun asked.[16]

Sun believed that China could avoid the class conflicts he had seen in the West. Indeed, in one sense China's underdevelopment was an advantage. Since the country had little industry, it had few factory workers and even fewer capitalists. Sun called for a policy that would encourage industry but avoid inequality. First, the republic's government should own all major industries, including railroads and large factories. That way profits would benefit the whole country—through better schools, for example—rather than enrich a few individuals. Second, Sun called for "equalization of land rights." He knew that as railroads spread and industry grew, the value of land went up. Sun proposed that China "capture" that increase. Imposing a high tax on rising property values "will prevent a few rich people from monopolizing favorably situated land," Sun believed, "yet it will not infringe on currently held wealth."[17] To avoid paying the tax, big landowners would sell land to peasants, so the plan would result in a fairer distribution of land.

Sun claimed that one of the inspirations for the Three Principles of the People was Abraham Lincoln's Gettysburg Address. He took Lincoln's call for a government "of the people" to mean nationalism, government "by the people" to signal democracy, and government "for the people" to refer to the common good or livelihood. The Three Principles may not have been great philosophy, but like Lincoln's speech, they framed the critical issues facing the nation at a turning point in its history. In later years, Sun redefined the principles in more radical terms.

A DECADE OF CHANGE

Although he still could not travel freely to China, Sun had a chance to inject his Three Principles into the impassioned discussions going on inside his homeland. The decade after 1900 saw an unprecedented wave of reform as the masters of the old empire realized the moment of truth had come at last. The Manchus pushed through more changes in the 10 years after the Boxer Rebellion than in the 60 years before it.

The most striking reforms touched education. The Manchus eliminated the 1,300-year-old civil service examination system in 1905, built over 50,000 new schools, adopted a modern curriculum, and sent Chinese students to study abroad, especially to nearby Japan. By 1905, over 8,000 Chinese students lived in Japan, many enrolled in military academies. The Manchus also modernized the army, and for the first time the military became an attractive career for ambitious young men. The empress dowager even promised that China would, at a future date, become a constitutional monarchy like Great Britain. "Never has so vast a population undergone so great an intellectual revolution in so short a time," the *New York Times* marveled in 1910.[18] An American naval officer who had spent years in China declared in 1911 that "the world can no longer consider China as an inert, non-receptive nation . . . hostile to all change."[19]

The reforms accelerated changes already underway in China's economy. Tripling the number of public school students created a more literate public, and as a result newspapers flourished. New social groups seemed to spring up overnight—teachers, journalists, entrepreneurs, and professional soldiers emerged as a new, educated middle class standing between peasants and government officials. Since these jobs had little status under China's ancient hierarchy of classes, the new middle class naturally favored change.

Ironically, the very reforms meant to preserve the empire helped to bury it. The Manchus had hoped that foreign-trained students would help modernize China and save the empire, but the plan backfired. Tokyo became an incubator for Chinese nationalism, and students and military cadets returned from Japan as rabid republicans. One popular student pamphlet illustrates their mood: "Kill! Kill! Kill! . . . Kill the foreign devils, kill the Christian converts who surrender to the foreign devils! If the Manchus help the foreigners kill us, then first kill all the Manchus. . . . Advance, kill! Advance, kill! Advance, kill!"[20] Students and army officers emerged as the revolution's strike force.

Although every one of the nearly dozen rebellions that he had sponsored had failed, Sun was still the best known of all anti-Manchu activists. In 1905, he arrived in Tokyo to stir the cauldron of student radicalism. The passage of time had convinced millions of Chinese that Sun had been right all along about the need for a republic, and the students and military cadets in Tokyo gave Sun a hero's welcome.

Like them, Sun saw China's weakness in stark relief against the remarkable modernization of Japan, driven home by the Japanese victory over Russia in 1905—the first time in modern history that an Asian nation had defeated a European power.

In this heady atmosphere, Sun rose before hundreds of Chinese students packed into a Tokyo restaurant in mid-August, 1905. Sun told the sweltering crowd what they wanted to hear—that with its vast resources, huge population, and long history of accomplishment China could leap into modernity even more quickly than Japan had done. The Three Principles of the People—nationalism, democracy, and livelihood—would light the way forward. "We are determined not to follow evolutionary change," Sun promised the youthful crowd, "but insist upon artificial change with its faster progress. I want you gentlemen to save China."[21] The students roared their approval.

While he was in Tokyo, Sun created a new revolutionary organization, the *Zhongguo Tongmenghui*, or Chinese Alliance. The goals of the Alliance closely followed his Three Principles of the People: to throw

Japan's victory over Russia in 1905, pictured here, inspired millions of Chinese who hoped to win the West's respect by forging a modern, powerful nation. After decades of arrogant treatment by the Great Powers, as one Japanese official put it, in just one year "we have managed to slay some 70,000 Europeans and behold! You accept us as 'civilized.'"

out the Manchus, create a republic, and equalize land rights. The new organization, however, had no more success than the earlier Society to Restore China's Prosperity in promoting revolution from outside China. In fact, Sun faced greater hurdles as the Manchus now aggressively pursued their enemies. Bowing to pressure from China, Japan expelled Sun in 1907; the following year, the French kicked Sun out of their colonies in Indochina. By 1911, the revolution's prospects seemed dim at best.

CREATING THE REPUBLIC

After so many failed uprisings, in the end the downfall of the Manchus came suddenly. It was fitting that anger at foreigners fired the powder keg. In 1911 the empire negotiated a large loan from European and American bankers, part of which would go to complete a railroad through Sichuan province. At first glance, this seemed patriotic— unlike most of the country's railroads, constructed under concessions, the new line would belong to China, not to foreigners. But in Sichuan, a wealthy elite had invested in the rail line and did not want to be bought out. They accused the Manchus of using foreign money to take over a Chinese enterprise, and by September peasants and workers joined in protests against the plan. Then, in October, a group of radicalized army officers rebelled and set up a military government in the nearby province of Hubei. With strong local support, they declared Hubei a republic and called on other provinces to secede from the empire. By December all of China's southern and central provinces had declared for the new republic.

Sun was traveling in the United States when he heard that a republic had been proclaimed. The rebels were not part of Sun's movement, yet they respected him enough to call him home to assume the new republic's presidency. Sun arrived in Shanghai on Christmas day, and a few days later he was elected interim president. In his first act, a symbolic one that signaled China's need to catch up with the rest of the world, Sun abolished the ancient Chinese calendar and adopted the modern Western calendar in its place. A few days later, he issued a republican manifesto in which he detailed all the reasons for overthrowing the Manchus, pledged that the new republic would respect foreigners and protect their property, and announced to the world "the entrance of China into the family of nations."[22] (See excerpts from the manifesto at the end of this chapter.)

Sun's dream of a republic had at last been realized, but the moment of euphoria was short-lived. A spellbinding orator and brilliant propagandist, Sun was not a talented executive. Since he had lived in exile for many years—he was only "half Chinese," his critics said—Sun was unfamiliar with China's internal politics. He soon realized that the nation he headed was sliding toward anarchy. Northern China had not joined the republic, and Sun feared that civil war between the north and south might break out, leading foreign powers to intervene and kill the republic before it had been properly born.

The most powerful figure in northern China was Yuan Shikai, a high imperial official and accomplished military leader. Unlike Sun, Yuan had the credentials to create a strong central government once he agreed to join the republic. In January 1912, in a step that amazed his compatriots and the world with its selflessness, Sun announced that he would turn over the presidency to Yuan Shikai. Sun encouraged all Chinese to unite around Yuan, who he said "is eminently fitted for the Presidency" and "is undoubtedly a great man worthy of support." As Sun gave up leadership of the republic he had dedicated his life to creating, the *Times* of London noted that he "has displayed personal dignity of a high order, and, though he has not displayed conspicuous gifts of statesmanship, he retires into privacy widely respected as a man and a patriot."[23]

DEVELOPING CHINA

In those first heady months, Sun believed that China had attained two of his People's Principles—nationalism (the Manchus abdicated on February 12, 1912) and democracy (Yuan Shikai promised to hold free elections under a new republican constitution). Sun now turned his energy to the third principle, livelihood. He had always believed that China needed to evolve economically to become a viable modern nation, and since the time of his letter to Li Hongzhang, Sun had said the key to economic growth was a modern rail system. When President Yuan offered to make him the head of a new railroad planning commission, Sun jumped at the chance to design China's future.

The United States, with the world's most productive industrial economy, had a rail network of over 320,000 kilometers (almost 200,000 miles), Sun pointed out, while China had only 9,000 kilometers of track. Sun busied himself drawing up a plan to build 90,000 kilometers of rail

Having resigned the presidency of China in 1912, Sun later battled against rival warlords to try to regain his leadership of the republic. "I am going to fight for humanity and civilization, republicanism and righteousness," he declared in 1922. (*Corbis*)

lines over 10 years, at a cost of over 1 billion dollars. The only conceivable source for such a vast sum of money was foreign capitalists. Sun knew that many of his compatriots opposed foreign investment in China—the overthrow of the Manchus had, after all, been triggered in part by anger over a foreign railroad loan. "I deeply believe that foreign loans will not harm the nation," Sun nevertheless argued in 1912. "When the subject of foreign loans is mentioned, we shun it like poison, without realizing that . . . foreign loans for productive purposes are beneficial."[24]

In February 1913 Sun traveled to Japan in search of capital for his grand railway plan. Sun's many friends in Japan welcomed him with banquets and receptions. As he met with government officials and potential investors, Sun made clear that he had boundless faith in Japan's goodwill toward China. Japan was his "second country," Sun told all who would listen, insisting that the new China would survive only with Japan's help.[25]

Sun's trip to Tokyo was the high point in his new role as economic modernizer. In reality, his railroad plan was impossibly ambitious for a nation already deep in debt. Moreover, he assumed that foreign capitalists would risk their money in China, even though it was obvious that most Chinese were hostile to foreign control of their railroads.

A SECOND REVOLUTION

The republic's golden age was painfully brief. In 1912, Sun's Chinese Alliance merged with four other groups to form the *Guomindang*, or Nationalist Party. In the republic's first free elections, the Guomindang won majorities in both houses of parliament. Yuan Shikai felt threatened by the Guomindang's strength and began to clip the wings of the fledgling democracy. Sun protested. Had he fought all those years to see the republic perish almost at birth? After Yuan executed two pro-Guomindang generals, Sun and other members of the party rose up against the government. "I recommended Yuan Shih-kai for the Presidency," Sun fumed, in the hope of achieving "the unification of the nation and the dawn of an era of peace and prosperity."[26] But now Yuan had betrayed the republic, and his command of the army allowed him to defeat what became a "second revolution." By August 1913, Sun was once again in exile, this time plotting against the president and the republic that he had helped put in place.

The next 10 years of China's history are often characterized as the warlord era. Yuan threw out the republic's constitution, imposed martial law, and banned the Guomindang. In 1915 he went further, recreating the empire with himself on the throne. Yuan died only three months later, and after his death China's government fractured, with no ruler able to control the whole nation. Sun returned to China and used Guangzhou (Canton) as a base for his drive to regain the presidency.

Soon enough, Sun was little different from the other warlords battling to rule China. His power rested on mercenary armies, whose pay was extracted from the people of Guangzhou through high taxes. Even so, Sun's modernizing goals did not entirely disappear. He invited Chinese graduates of American universities to Guangzhou, which despite nearly constant warfare became a showcase for material progress. "The Canton Government includes many able young Chinese and has done some good work in its own province," the *Times* of London admitted in 1922. "Some foreign observers regard Canton as the best and most hopeful element in China to-day."[27]

UNLIKELY ANTI-IMPERIALIST

Of all China's nationalist leaders, Sun had always been the least hostile to foreigners. He hoped that China could benefit from foreign investment while avoiding domination by the industrial powers, and he had a naive faith in Japan's good intentions. But Japan's victories over China and Russia, in 1895 and 1905, respectively, had strengthened the hand of militarists who wanted to create an East Asian empire to rival Europe's empires. Despite the goodwill of some Japanese, the government in Tokyo clearly had designs on its huge but weak neighbor. In January 1915, two years after Sun's visit to Tokyo and with Europe embroiled in World War I, Japan presented China with the infamous Twenty-one Demands, which expanded Japanese influence in China, especially in the north. Across China, patriots burned the Japanese flag. Sun's openness to foreigners thus put him at odds with many of his own people.

After 1919, however, even Sun found himself in conflict with foreign powers. At the Versailles Conference that ended World War I, Woodrow Wilson promised to protect the rights of less-developed countries. The Chinese assumed this meant that Germany's sphere of influence in northern China, which Japan had seized in 1914, would be returned to them. On May 4, 1919, word reached China that the Versailles Conference had allowed Japan to keep the territory. Student demonstrators again burned Japanese flags in Beijing. The *May 4 Movement*, a new stage in Chinese nationalism, denounced Western hypocrisy and called for a firm anti-imperialist policy.

In the aftermath of the May 4 Movement, no Chinese leader could avoid the issue of foreign power and foreign money. Europeans, Japanese, and Americans controlled many key industries and institutions in China. Most controversial of all, the main source of Chinese government revenue—custom duties charged on imports—had been in foreign hands since the 1800s. One of Sun's last political battles was with the customs service.

Guangzhou, or Canton, was Sun's base of civil and military power, but the revenue that the foreign-controlled customs service collected there went to his rivals in Beijing, with whom he was at war. Sun appealed to the foreign officials to allow him to keep the funds collected at Guangzhou. When they refused, he appealed directly to the American people for support. "We must stop that money from going to Peking [Beijing] to buy arms to kill us," Sun declared, "just as your forefathers stopped taxation going to English coffers by throwing English tea into Boston Harbour."[28] Despite the plea, American and European warships arrived in Guangzhou harbor to keep Sun from seizing control of the custom house there. Though he was defeated, Sun's willingness to stand up to the foreigners won him widespread respect across China.[29]

REDEFINING THE THREE PRINCIPLES

Sun never gave up hope of cooperation with the United States and Europe. As late as 1919 he wrote a book in English, *The International Development of China*, which once again tried to entice American and European capitalists to invest in China's railways, roads, mines, ports, and other infrastructure. Despite this overture, the reality of his situation pushed Sun in a new direction. By the 1920s, he had changed the emphasis of the Three Principles. The disastrous implosion of China's first republican government led Sun to pay less attention to nationalism and democracy. He focused increasingly on livelihood, the material well-being of the people. In the violent political conflicts of the early 1920s, Sun began to connect his Third Principle more explicitly with socialism.

When Sun first developed the Three Principles in the early 1900s, socialism was still only a theory—no nation had yet embraced it. Then, in 1917, the Russian Revolution toppled the tsar, and by the early 1920s Vladimir Lenin and his fellow Bolsheviks had created the world's first Communist government. (At the time, the terms *Communism* and *socialism* were used interchangeably—thus the *Communist* Party controlled the Union of Soviet *Socialist* Republics.) Eager for allies, the

Bolsheviks took a great interest in China's seething instability, seeing their populous neighbor as a potential ally against Western imperialism. Many Chinese, in turn, admired the triumph of the Bolsheviks. Lenin had succeeded where Sun Yatsen had failed: By 1923 the Bolsheviks had a firm grip on power and ruled a united Russia, whereas China's revolution had resulted in fragmentation and chaos.

After his conflict with the customs service, Sun began to echo Lenin's declarations against the West's imperialism. "We Asiatics must emancipate Asia and the down-trodden States," he announced in 1924, " . . . from European and American oppression." While "other powers aim at dominating the so-called weak nations," Sun noted, Russia does not.[30] Sun had a special reason to look favorably on the Soviet Union, since it was the only Western country that recognized him as ruler of all China. "If we wish our revolution to succeed," he now argued, "we must learn the methods, organization and training of the Russians."[31]

Sun made good on this pledge. With advice from Soviet advisors in Guangzhou, he "reformed" the Guomindang, giving nearly all decision-making power to party leaders, himself in particular. The new structure closely followed Lenin's model for the Bolshevik Party, which exerted dictatorial power in the Soviet Union.

Sun was far from being an orthodox Communist, given that he believed China could avoid the "class struggle" between workers and capitalists that Marxists said was inevitable. When his Soviet advisors urged Sun to make his movement more radical, he resisted. When they pleaded with him to seize land from the landlords and give it to the peasants to win their support, Sun refused. He did not believe the economic program of the Communists could work in an overwhelmingly peasant nation like China. Even so, he allowed members of the Communist Party to join the Guomindang. But to make clear his basic disagreement with Marxism, he issued a public statement declaring that "the Communist order . . . cannot actually be introduced into China, because there do not exist here the conditions for the successful establishment of either Communism or Sovietism."[32]

Although Sun did not become a Communist, it is significant that he found common ground with the Soviet Union in opposing Western imperialism. History would prove that Sun was wrong about the impossibility of establishing Communism in China. In the 1930s, under Mao Zedong, the Communist Party expropriated land and thereby succeeded in winning widespread peasant support, a crucial factor in Mao's victory in 1949.

The conflict between the Guomindang and the Communist Party would not be settled in Sun's lifetime. In 1924, the 58-year-old Sun was diagnosed with cancer of the liver. He settled in Beijing, where he died in March 1925. On his deathbed, he urged the Chinese people to follow his program for the future as outlined in his *Three Principles of the People* and other writings.

CONCLUSION

Sun Yatsen was an unlikely candidate to be the "father of his country." For most of his life he lived either on the European fringe of China or the Chinese fringe of Europe, Southeast Asia, and the United States, yet Sun never doubted his mission to forge a new China or his ability to represent the men and women of China. Time after time his efforts failed, yet Sun recovered and tried again.

Sun's legend and popularity were powerful enough that all political factions laid claim to his legacy. In 1927, the Guomindang purged its Communist members, and for the next 20 years the two parties waged a civil war for control of China. The Guomindang, led by Sun's protégé Chiang Kai-shek (in Pinyin Romanization Jiang Jieshi), canonized Sun and made his writings, especially the *Three Principles of the People*, into sacred texts for the party. They remain so today for the government of Taiwan. The Communists gave Sun credit for leading China through its transformation from empire to republic, which they saw as a necessary stage before the leap from capitalism to socialism. Today over 40 Zhongshan Parks in honor of Sun Zhongshan, as the Chinese know him, dot the People's Republic of China. One of the most beautiful is in the heart of Beijing, next to the old imperial palace complex known as the Forbidden City.

In more concrete terms, Sun's legacy was mixed. His reorganization of the Guomindang along Soviet lines squelched internal debate and gave the party a top-down structure. That change meant that neither of China's major parties, the Guomindang or the Communists, was democratic. Still, Sun played a key role in making old China into a modern republic. His commitment to economic justice inspires many Chinese today as their nation's rapid economic growth creates millionaires while relegating hundreds of millions of peasants to abject poverty.

SOURCES

■ Sun Yatsen Pleads for Reform, 1894

In 1894, Sun took the bold step of carrying a letter of advice to Li Hongzhang (1823–1901), a champion of self-strengthening in the Manchu dynasty. For the son of a peasant to address one of the empire's most powerful officials was almost unthinkable, and Li did not grant him an audience. Later, Sun had the letter published, a step on his way to becoming an open opponent of the Manchu regime.

As you read, evaluate the changes that Sun Yatsen advocated. In which four areas did he say China must follow the West? How, according to Sun, would reform in each area make China stronger? Do you think the changes Sun urges could have been made within China's imperial structure? Why or why not?

While young, I studied abroad, where I acquainted myself with the written and spoken languages of the Western countries and with their politics, government, and customs, along with astronomy, geography, chemistry, and general science. I tried especially to learn how these countries had grown rich and strong and how they had civilized their people. . . . I have often wanted to submit to you, who are in authority, my humble opinions regarding the overall political situation. However, because of my humble position and the consequent insignificance of my remarks, I have not dared to do so. On the other hand, lately I have observed the state's vigorous efforts to chart a course to enrich and strengthen the nation. . . . I assume, therefore, that you gentlemen in authority have already pondered what we must do to maintain domestic tranquility as well as enrich the nation and strengthen its military power. . . .

I am keenly aware that the wealth and power of the European nations are the result not only of their having ships and powerful guns, strong fortresses and formidable troops but also because their people can fully employ their talents, their land can be fully utilized, their natural resources can be fully tapped, and their goods can freely flow. These four elements are the basis of a nation's wealth and strength and the root of good government. . . . If instead of urgently addressing these four issues,

---

Source: Reprinted from *Prescriptions for Saving China: Selected Writings of Sun Yat-sen,* edited by Julie Lee Wei, Ramon H. Myers, and Donald G. Gillin, with the permission of the publisher, Hoover Institution Press. Translation copyright 1994 by the Board of Trustees of the Leland Stanford Junior University.

we merely concentrate on building strong ships and powerful guns, we will be ignoring the root and seeking the flower. . . .

Since ancient times, China has been peerless in the breadth and depth of its system of education. Unfortunately, that system has fallen into disrepair . . . Meanwhile, the modern age has witnessed the sudden emergence of the Western countries. . . . Their schools are everywhere in their countries, and their people, rich or poor, are diligent in the pursuit of knowledge. . . . Everyone in the nation begins his studies in early childhood. . . . In the West a man who has even the slightest talent will be cherished by being given a specialty. Consequently, everyone strives of his own accord. . . . Such encouragement is the reason for the West's continual advances in various fields of learning. . . .

Thus, given the right education, there will be no waste of talent; . . . given the right system of appointment and employment, there will be no place for people to gain undeserved promotions to high office. . . . Then we need not worry about whether the nation will become strong and wealthy; it will happen as a matter of course. . . .

Agriculture in China today has been increasingly neglected. The farmers only know how to cling to traditional ways and do not know how to adjust to change . . . People toil much but gain little, and feeding the people is increasingly difficult. . . . The countries of the great West are keenly aware that the great source of wealth lies in not wasting the land. . . . In those countries, everything that is good for agriculture is promoted and everything that is harmful to it is removed. . . . Once agriculture is enlightened, the productivity of the same patch of land will multiply several times, which amounts to transforming one acre of land into several acres and enlarging one country into the size of several countries. Consequently, although the size of the population may increase several times, the threat of famine need no longer exist. That is why I advocate the speedy creation of agricultural schools.

After . . . agricultural science is developed, we must have sophisticated machinery if we are to save labor and accelerate production. . . . Ever since ancient times, plowing has been done with the labor of oxen and horses; in modern times, however, animals have largely been replaced by ever-more sophisticated machines, which do more work at less cost. . . .

In the great West, educated people regard science and its application as the basis for providing people with a good life . . . Consequently, they devote themselves daily to the study of the laws of nature and their application. . . . Electricity . . . is already used worldwide to provide light and send telegrams; . . . In the future, electricity will surely replace coal in driving machinery. . . . All this suggests that the more we seek to use matter, the less we have to use human labor.

Certainly the day will come when man will need only to use his mind and not his muscle, and machines will do all his work for him. . . .

In the West, goods flow freely, merchants proliferate, wealth is constantly increasing, and its nations grow ever stronger. In China, things are different. There are customs stations at every provincial border, so that even after taxes have been paid at the port of entry, further taxes are imposed everywhere. Consequently, there are obstructions everywhere. . . . Because of all this, merchants feel as if they have bound feet . . . Yet, commerce and shipping are a major way for people to create wealth. "When the people have enough, how can their ruler not have enough? If the people do not have enough, how can their ruler have enough?"[33] . . . . Skimming the fat from the common people is no benefit to the national economy or the people's livelihood. . . .

In the West the interests of state and those of commerce flourish together; . . . The reason why Britain can conquer India, control Southeast Asia, seize Africa and annex Australia is because of its commercial strength. National defense cannot function without money, and money for the military will not accumulate without commerce. . . . Ever since China began trading with the West, all the privileges and profits of that trade have been seized by the West. Why is this so? It is because they have been protecting their commerce, while we have not. On the contrary, we have been robbing our merchants, impoverishing them, and constricting and repressing them. . . . Several hundred years ago, the land of America was just as vast as it is today. Why is it now rich and then poor? It is because America places value on having merchants engaging in trade and promoting the circulation of goods. . . . If one is intent on strengthening the nation, how can one fail to take immediate steps?

■ Sun Yatsen Issues the Republican Manifesto, 1912

A few days after his election as acting president of the new Chinese Republic in December 1911, Sun Yatsen issued the following manifesto, justifying the overthrow of the Manchus and setting out the basic principles of the new republic. According to Sun, what justified the revolution? Compare this document with the American Declaration of Independence in 1776. Do you think Sun was consciously echoing the American document? If so, in what way or ways? Which statements in the manifesto were probably meant to reassure foreigners about China's new government? On balance, how would you characterize this manifesto—radical, conservative, or something else?

To all friendly nations,—Greeting. . . . We now proclaim . . . the establishment of a Republic. The substitution of a Republic for a Monarchy is not the fruit of transient passion but the natural outcome of a long-cherished desire for freedom, contentment, and advancement. . . . We have borne our grievance for 267 years with patience. . . . Oppressed beyond human endurance we deemed it our inalienable right, as well as a sacred duty, to appeal to arms to deliver ourselves and our posterity from the yoke to which we have for so long been subjected. . . . The policy of the Manchus has been one of unequivocal seclusion and unyielding tyranny. . . . Now we submit to the free peoples of the world the reasons justifying the revolution and the inauguration of the present Government.

Prior to the usurpation of the throne by the Manchus the land was open to foreign intercourse and religious tolerance existed. . . . Dominated by ignorance and selfishness the Manchus closed the land to the outer world. . . . The Manchus have governed the country to the lasting injury and detriment of the people, creating privileges and monopolies, erecting about themselves barriers of exclusion . . . which have been rigorously maintained for centuries. They have levied irregular and hurtful taxes without the consent of the people, and have restricted foreign trade to Treaty Ports. They have . . . obstructed internal commerce, retarded the creation of industrial enterprises, [and] rendered impossible the development of natural resources. . . . They have . . . rejected the most reasonable demands for better government, and reluctantly conceded so-called reforms under the most urgent pressure, promising without any intention of fulfilling. They have failed to appreciate the anguish-causing lessons taught them by foreign Powers, and . . . have brought themselves and our people beneath the contempt of the world.

Revolutionary Pledges

A remedy of these evils will render possible the entrance of China into the family of nations. . . . We publicly and unreservedly declare the following to be our promises: —

. . . . Foreign loans and indemnities incurred by the Manchus before the Revolution will be acknowledged. Payments made to loans incurred by the Manchus after its commencement will be repudiated. Concessions granted to nations and their nationals before the Revolution will

---

Source: From Herbert A. Giles, *China and the Manchus,* available at Project Gutenberg; http://www.gutenberg.org/ebooks/2156.

be respected. Any and all granted after it will be repudiated. The persons and property of foreign nationals within the jurisdiction of the Republic will be respected and protected. . . . Manchus who abide peacefully in the limits of our jurisdiction will be accorded equality and given protection.

We will remodel the laws, revise the civil, criminal, commercial, and mining codes, reform the finances, abolish restrictions on trade and commerce, and insure religious toleration and the cultivation of better relations with foreign peoples and Governments than have ever been maintained before. . . .

With this message of peace and good will the Republic cherishes the hope of being admitted into the family of nations, not merely to share its rights and privileges, but to co-operate in the great and noble task of building up the civilization of the world.

Sun Yat Sen, President

■ Sun Yatsen Explains the Principle of Livelihood, 1912

For a fleeting moment from late December 1911 to January 1912, Sun emerged as president of the new Chinese republic. It was in the context of those heady days that Sun delivered this speech on economic development in China.

As the previous documents show, Sun believed China needed to emulate the West in many areas. Here, however, he criticizes the growing gap between rich and poor in Europe and the United States. What were the consequences of that gap in Western nations? What advantages does China enjoy over industrialized nations in pursuing the well-being of the people? Compare this speech with Sun's letter to Li Hongzhang (page 113). What differences do you note? Are there also significant continuities in Sun's thinking? Explain.

The Manchu dynasty has now abdicated the throne and the Republic of China has been created. The two principles of nationalism and democracy have been attained. Only the principle of livelihood is left to be addressed, and it should be the focus of our future efforts. . . . Today

---

Source: Reprinted from *Prescriptions for Saving China: Selected Writings of Sun Yat-sen,* edited by Julie Lee Wei, Ramon H. Myers, and Donald G. Gillin, with the permission of the publisher, Hoover Institution Press. Translation copyright 1994 by the Board of Trustees of the Leland Stanford Junior University.

many people's idea of reforming China is merely to turn China into an extremely strong and rich country, the equal of Europe and America. But they are actually wrong. Today, no nation is richer or stronger than England and America, none more civilized than France. . . . They have achieved admirable forms of government, yet their poor and rich classes are still too far apart. . . . When only a minority consisting of capitalists can enjoy the good life, while the majority of workers must endure hardship, they will naturally not be able to live together in peace and harmony. . . . In England, America and other countries, because their civilizations are advanced and their industry and commerce are well developed, a social revolution is difficult to achieve. China's civilization is not advanced, its industry and commerce are not developed. . . . Since there are not many middle-class families, and even fewer capitalist families like those in other countries, effecting a social revolution would not be a painful process. But we should not put aside a social revolution just because the evils of capitalism have not yet appeared. . . . If we think that we . . . will address the question only after the populace has reached a high level of education and rich and poor classes have formed, then it will be too late. It is just because countries like England and America did not pay attention to this in the past that they are suffering the consequences at present . . . If we . . . fail to think of preventing misfortunes, then later, when the capitalists emerge, their oppressive methods will, I fear, be worse than those of autocratic monarchs. . . .

If we could succeed in equalizing land rights, then we would have accomplished 70 or 80 percent of the social revolution. . . . In the past, people paid taxes on their land based on the size of the holding. . . . In the future, we should reform this system into one, taxing according to price. . . . To collect tax according to acreage of land brings you to the inequality of land rights. . . . So the best way is to enact a law to assess taxes ad valorem [based on value, not acreage]. . . . This sort of taxation based on value is already in effect in England. . . .

To seek out foreign credit for the sake of engaging in nonproductive activities is harmful, whereas to seek out foreign credit for the sake of engaging in productive activities is beneficial. America's progress and prosperity, South America's, Argentina's, and Japan's buoyant economies, are all thanks to foreign credit. . . . Last year when I was passing through Canada, I saw Chinese workers using machines to dig coal in coal mines. Each person could excavate more than ten tons a day. . . . In the interior of China, a worker in a coal mine digs less than a ton a day. His productivity is very low. If he could dig with machines, his productivity would increase more than tenfold, which means that wealth would increase more than tenfold. Wouldn't that make us one of the richest nations in the world?. . . .

While we are endeavoring to make the nation rich and strong, we should at the same time take measures to prevent the monopolistic abuses of capitalists. And there is no way to prevent such abuses other than by socialism. . . . Germany today is using such policies, whereby the big industries of the nation such as railways, electricity and water supplies must all be nationalized and cannot be privately owned. . . . We should learn from Germany. . . .

We must adopt national social polices so that society will not suffer from oppression by certain economic classes but will follow the natural and inevitable course in achieving appropriate progress. The path to what we call "a rich nation and a prosperous people" is no more than this.

■ A Picture of Rural Life in China

The postcard below, like those from Korea and China reproduced in the introduction to this book, was printed by Westerners curious about premodern peoples. Here, a family of Chinese peasants stands in front of their home showing the tools and utensils they use in their daily life.

From the picture, what do you think the family did for a living? Of what materials are the tools and receptacles made? How is the house constructed? Do any of the objects in the picture appear to have been made by machines in a factory, as opposed to being produced by artisans or made at home? How many metal objects are evident? How

Chinese Peasants.

wealthy do you think this family was? Although posed, do you think this photograph accurately reflects rural life in China? Explain.

NOTES

1. Quoted in Lyon Sharman, *Sun Yat-sen: His Life and Its Meaning* (Hamden, CT: Archon, 1965), p. 96.

2. John King Fairbank, *Great Chinese Revolution, 1800–1985* (New York: Harper & Row, 1987), p. 2.

3. J. A. G. Roberts, *A Concise History of China* (Cambridge, MA: Harvard University, 1999), p. 185.

4. The term is used by Michael Gasster in "The Republican Revolutionary Movement," in John K. Fairbank and Kwang-Ching Liu, eds., *Cambridge History of China*, vol. II (New York: Cambridge, 1980), p. 466.

5. Quoted in Sharman, *Sun Yat-sen*, p. 67.

6. Fairbank, *Great Chinese Revolution*, p. 119.

7. Sharman, *Sun Yat-sen*, p. 36.

8. Quoted in Sharman, *Sun Yat-sen*, p. 48.

9. "Plan Behind China Revolt Is Revealed," *New York Times*, October 14, 1911, p. 1.

10. Sharman, *Sun Yat-sen*, p. 63.

11. Fairbank, *Great Chinese Revolution*, p. 138.

12. *New York Times*, October 14, 1900, p. 6.

13. Ibid.

14. "Topics of the Times," *New York Times*, May 23, 1897, p. 6.

15. Quoted in Sharman, *Sun Yat-sen*, p. 4.

16. Quoted in Harold Schiffrin, "Sun Yat-sen's Early Land Policy: The Origin and Meaning of 'Equalization of Land Rights,' " *Journal of Asian Studies* 16: 4 (August 1957), pp. 551, 552.

17. Ibid., p. 554.

18. "China's Awakening Shown Throughout the Country," *New York Times*, September 4, 1910, p. SM 11.

19. "Gen. Greely Analyzes the Great Awakening of China," *New York Times*, October 1, 1911, p. SM 9.

20. Quoted in Gasster, "The Republican Revolutionary Movement," p. 481.

21. Schiffrin, *Sun Yat-sen*, p. 107.

22. "Anarchy in Szechuan," *Times* (London), January 6, 1912, p. 6.

23. "Sun Yat-sen in Peking," *Times* (London), August 26, 1912, p. 6; "Imperial and Foreign Intelligence," *Times* (London), April 2, 1912, p. 5.

24. A. James Gregor and Maria Hsia Chang, "Marxism, Sun Yat-sen, and the Concept of 'Imperialism,' " *Pacific Affairs* 55: 1 (Spring 1982), p. 69.

25. "Sun Yat-Sen's Visit to Japan," *Times* (London), March 22, 1913, p. 5.

26. "Position of the President," *Times* (London), May 3, 1913, p. 7.

27. "China's Rival War Lords," *Times* (London), May 1, 1922, p. 21.

28. "The Canton Customs," *Times* (London), December 20, 1923, p. 11.

29. C. Martin Wilbur, *Sun Yat-sen, Frustrated Patriot* (New York: Columbia University, 1976), pp. 183–187.

30. "Dr. Sun Sees a Free Asia," *New York Times*, December 1, 1924, p. 3.

31. Quoted in Schiffrin, *Sun Yat-sen*, p. 242.

32. Wilbur, *Sun Yat-sen*, p. 137.

33. A quotation from Book XII of the *Analects*, a collection of statements ascribed to Confucius and his students. The *Analects* was one of the four classics that formed the basis of the civil service examination material during the Ming and Qing eras.

Mustafa Kemal:
Muslim Modernity

In the dark days that followed the end of World War I, the Ottoman Empire teetered on the brink of destruction. The Ottoman government had thrown in with Germany when war erupted in 1914. Now, in defeat, the sultan (as the Ottoman emperor was called) faced the anger and ambition of the Allies who occupied most of his empire. The massacre of more than 1 million Armenian civilians during the war had convinced many Europeans that the Ottomans should not "govern Christians, Jews or any non-Moslems," and justified their plan to carve the empire up among themselves. Desperate to preserve his domain, the sultan admitted that "unfortunate" wartime events placed Turks in an "unfavorable light" but argued that the Ottoman nation should be judged "by its long history rather than by a single period."

The Allies, meeting in Versailles to plan the postwar world, sternly rejected the sultan's claim for complete territorial restoration and denounced the history of Turkish rule over "her heterogeneous empire."[1] They presented the sultan with a peace treaty that left him with only a tiny fraction of his prewar lands. The sultan accepted the humiliating Treaty of Sevres in 1920 and ordered his army to surrender their weapons to the European occupiers.

What happened next took the world by surprise. Among the Ottoman generals sent to carry out the surrender was Mustafa Kemal (1881–1938). Instead of obeying the sultan, he led the Turkish people in a multi-front war to expel the Europeans. Defeating the foreign armies and creating a Turkish republic would have guaranteed Kemal a large place in history, but his real achievements came later. As Turkey's first elected president, he pushed through reforms that modernized every aspect of Turkish life. The rapid changes astonished Western observers, who declared that Kemal had taken "a slice of Asia and tried to turn it into a bit of Europe."[2]

Mustafa Kemal's transformation of Turkey is the most thoroughgoing case of defensive modernization examined in this book. To this day, the man who in 1934 was honored by his country with the name Atatürk, "Father of the Turks," is omnipresent in Turkey—every coin and bill carries his image and his alone. While many Turks revere him, however, others now denounce him as an enemy of the Muslim faith. Kemal's legacy in Turkey begs the question: Does modernization automatically mean Westernization? As we shall see, the answer is far from simple.

EUROPE'S "OTHER"

Unlike China, located thousands of miles from Europe, the Ottoman Empire had been not merely on Europe's doorstep but actually in its living room, so to speak, for over 500 years. The Ottomans surged into Europe's consciousness in the 1300s as they pushed their empire westward, eventually capturing Constantinople, the ancient city that was renamed Istanbul in the 20th century. Even at this early date Ottoman power reverberated across Europe: Conquering Istanbul in 1453 gave Sultan Mehmed II control of the main trading route from Europe to Central and South Asia. It was the search for an alternative route to the spice islands of Asia that motivated Portuguese and Spanish exploration down the west coast of Africa and far into the Atlantic.

The Ottomans continued to expand westward in the 1500s from Anatolia, the large peninsula created by the Black and Marmara seas to the north and the Aegean and Mediterranean to the west and south. Eventually their empire encompassed a large swath of the Balkans, the area of southeastern Europe that includes modern Greece, Albania, Serbia, Romania, Macedonia, and Bulgaria. Ottoman armies also marched south to conquer much of the Persian Gulf and Arabian Peninsula, as well as Egypt, Libya, and Tunisia in North Africa. By 1600 there was no larger or more formidable empire west of China than that of the Ottomans.

Over the next three centuries, the Ottoman Empire became a major player in Europe's balance of power, occasionally in alliance but often at war with the continent's kings, emperors, and princes. On two occasions—first in 1529, then in 1683—Ottoman armies besieged Vienna in the heart of Central Europe. As a powerful but non-Christian empire, the Ottomans loomed large in European art, literature, and political thought. Muslim characters appear as counterpoints to Christians in the works of Shakespeare, Cervantes, Montesquieu, Voltaire, Goethe, Flaubert, and Byron, among others.

The second assault on Vienna in 1683 turned out to be the high-water mark of Ottoman power in Europe. By the early 1700s, the changes that would propel Europe into the Industrial Revolution had made European armies consistently superior to the Ottomans. In wars against the neighboring empires of Austria and Russia, the sultan's troops met defeat after defeat. In the 1840s, Britain forced the empire to lower its tariffs and thus permit European manufactured goods to undercut the products made by Ottoman artisans. European investors also pumped money into the empire, so much money that one financial historian declared that there was no other sovereign nation in the world "where the influence of foreign capital was greater than in the Ottoman Empire."[3] French, British, and German capitalists controlled key sectors of the economy through concessions for banks, railroads, ports, mines, and oil wells. After the empire defaulted on its loans, the foreign creditors set up a public debt administration in 1881. A committee of Europeans now controlled the Muslim empire's finances. As in China, the Ottoman Empire remained technically independent, even as it was increasingly dominated, politically and economically, by Europe.

EARLY EFFORTS AT REFORM

In the 1790s, a well-educated and open-minded sultan, Selim III, took the now familiar first step in modernization by trying to improve the empire's army and navy. Selim brought French advisers to Istanbul and created new military colleges to train officers. His goal was to build a new army to replace the *janissaries,* an elite force created centuries earlier to protect the sultan. Over time, the janissaries had won many privileges and at times even deposed sultans they did not like. Naturally, Selim's plan to build a modern army threatened the janissaries, while conservatives objected to the fact that Christian officers now gave orders to Muslim soldiers. In 1807, the janissaries supported a rebellion that overthrew Selim, who was killed the following year.

The conservatives had won, but reform was not dead. Sultan Mahmud II took the throne in 1808 and pushed ahead with modernization despite the unhappy fate of his cousin, Selim III. In the 1820s the Ottoman army suffered another stinging defeat when Greece won its independence from the empire. This time Mahmud II rallied his people against the janissaries with the aim of creating a new imperial army. In 1826 the janissaries revolted, but the rebellion was suppressed with great bloodshed; thousands of the warriors were massacred or later executed, and the survivors exiled. The Janissary Corps, founded in the 14th century, was no more. With the *Tanzimat* (reorganization) Decree of 1839, reform moved beyond the military to promise equal rights for all Ottoman subjects, Christians and Jews, as well as Muslims. From the Tanzimat Decree through the 1870s, political and economic changes moved ahead rapidly. The first Turkish-language newspaper began publication in Istanbul in 1840; the empire's first railroad opened in 1866, and telegraph service spread across the empire by the 1860s. Foreign investors and Ottoman Christians played leading roles in these technological leaps.

The need to reform the empire was not purely a reaction to Western pressure. Corruption, inefficiency, and decay had worried the sultans and their ruling elites well before the 19th century. Kemal Karpat notes that Ottoman society was "subject to transformation through the impact of internal forces long before massive European influence."[4] Nevertheless, humiliating military defeats and demoralizing economic dependency gave urgency to the reforms.

As in China, reform triggered resistance. In the Ottoman case, the strongest opposition came from the religious hierarchy, the *ulema.* These religious scholars played an important role in the Ottoman state, controlling nearly all schools and serving as judges who enforced *şeriat,* religious laws derived from the Quran that govern all aspects of Muslim life. Given the important role of the ulema in both areas, any attempt to reform education or the legal system was bound to become a religious conflict.

Political reform also prompted a backlash. Muslims saw the empire as the protector of their faith—after all, the sultan was also *caliph,* the spiritual leader of Sunni Islam worldwide. Since the sultan thus embodied church and state in his person, how could the two ever be separated, as many European states were attempting to do? And how could *infidels*, as non-Muslims were pejoratively called, have equal rights within a state dedicated to protecting Islam? As in China, the sultan and his circle also worried that even small steps toward democracy—for example, accepting a constitution that limited the sultan's power—would put the empire on the road to extinction. Nevertheless, in 1876 Sultan Abdulhamid II did accept a written constitution that created a parliament, the first representative body in Ottoman history.

Once more the leap forward prompted a step backward. When legislators met in 1877, they gently challenged the sultan's authority. Abdulhamid responded by dissolving parliament, suspending the constitution, and clamping down on newspapers. For the next 30 years, opposition to the old regime went underground.

REFORMING A MULTICULTURAL EMPIRE

Reformers in the Ottoman Empire faced issues that Sun Yatsen in China did not. Unlike the Chinese Empire, which despite its vast size and various minorities, was relatively homogeneous in language and culture at its core, the Ottomans ruled over very different peoples in North Africa, the Middle East, and the Balkans. Turkish-speakers dominated Anatolia, but there were large numbers of Kurds, Greeks, and Armenians as well. Religious differences also abounded. In the Arabic-speaking south nearly all subjects were Muslims, although there were pockets of Arab Christians. In the Balkans, Christians were a majority, while Greeks and Armenians made up some 20 percent of Anatolia's population. The Ottomans had normally not persecuted those who did not share their faith. Nevertheless, the empire's many different Christian denominations, as well as Jews, were distinct groups that lived in their own communities, paid special taxes, had their own laws and courts, and even wore special clothing.

Could a single government hold together a region that stretched from the pyramids of Egypt to Mount Olympus in Macedonia, from Algeria to Azerbaijan? Did the polyglot, multi-ethnic, and multi-faith Ottoman state have enough internal glue to develop into a modern nation? The Ottomanists, as they came to be called, hoped so. They envisioned an empire in which Muslims, Christians, and Jews had equal rights and pledged loyalty to the central government. Like the leaders of China's "self-strengthening" movement, they hoped to modernize the empire in order to preserve it.

Other reformers felt the multi-ethnic model was doomed to fail. The future, these nationalists said, belonged to nation-states made up of people who shared the same language, religion, culture, and history. How could Christians in Macedonia, Muslims in Libya, and Jews in Istanbul identify with the same government? Events in southern Europe in the late 1800s seemed to confirm the nationalists' vision of the future. Independence movements led by Christians in Serbia, Bulgaria, and elsewhere in the Balkans threatened to dismember the empire.

Another group, the Islamists, believed that religion could hold the empire together. Fellow Muslims from Egypt to Bosnia could be rallied around the sultan in his role as caliph, a title and office claimed by the sultans since the mid-1500s. The conservative Abdulhamid II promoted this idea. Nevertheless, many devout Muslims in Egypt, Iraq, Syria, and elsewhere wanted their own nation-states and refused to defer to a ruler who could not even speak Arabic. In the end, it seemed that no gravitational force was strong enough to hold the empire's distant and diverse regions in orbit around Istanbul.

Even in its last years the sprawling Ottoman Empire spread far beyond Anatolia to include all or most of modern-day Israel, Jordan, Syria, Iraq, Saudi Arabia, and the Persian Gulf States.

THE RISE OF MUSTAFA KEMAL

As debates raged about the future of the declining empire, the man who would eventually lay that empire to rest was born in Salonika (present-day Thessaloniki in Greece) in 1881 with the sole name of Mustafa, as was the custom of the time. Salonika, a busy port on the Aegean Sea in eastern Macedonia, was part of the empire's multicultural fringe, far from the Anatolian heartland. Mustafa spent his formative years among a population with a Jewish majority and a large Christian minority, mostly Greek. His family lived in a middle-class Turkish neighborhood, and his father Ali Rıza worked as a customs official for the empire.

Ali Rıza had little interest in religion and, indeed, favored the progressive ideas that were then filtering into the empire. Mustafa's mother, like most Turkish women of the time, was deeply religious and scarcely able to read or write. She longed for Mustafa to attend a *medrese*, or religious school, and become a scholar by memorizing the Quran in Arabic—a language he could not speak or understand. Ali Rıza won out, and Mustafa registered at a new school led by a man renowned as a critical thinker.

From an early age Mustafa showed a strong will and an aptitude for hard work. Pushed in part by his mother's total dedication to his success, he came to believe he was destined for greatness. "I don't mean to be like the rest of you," he told his schoolmates in Salonika. When the boy was eight, his father died after a long illness. Unable to afford to live in town, the family moved to a farm near the village of Rapla. There Mustafa learned about peasant life firsthand, chasing crows away from crops and hauling firewood. His time in Rapla would help him to understand the country people who made up the vast majority of Turkey's population.

Rapla had no schools that suited Mustafa, so his mother reluctantly sent him back to Salonika to live with his great aunt. Enrolled at a new institution, Mustafa soon locked horns with the headmaster, a traditionalist well known for the savage beatings he gave his students. After coming home bloody and bruised one day, Mustafa had had enough. A relative arranged for him to apply to a local military school. Without telling his family, he took the entrance test and passed. "My mother was afraid of the military," Mustafa later wrote, "and was against me becoming a soldier."[5] Since the empire was often at war, a soldier's life was dangerous. Faced with her son's ferociously strong will, however, she gave the plan her blessing.

Mustafa was a good student who excelled in mathematics. Indeed, his math teacher was so impressed that he gave Mustafa a second name, *Kemal*, which means "perfection" in Turkish. Mustafa Kemal did well enough at the academy to go on with his military training at Monastir military institute, about 80 miles from Salonika. There his intellectual world broadened. A good friend, Ömer Naci, gave him Turkish literature, which Kemal had never looked at before. "I found poetry fascinating," he recalled, but officers at the school told him to "forget about becoming a poet, because it is going to prevent you from becoming a fine soldier."[6] Kemal obeyed, but his love for the rhythms and imagery of poetry helped make him a powerful, persuasive orator, a key factor in his later success as a political leader.

From Monastir, Mustafa Kemal went on to officer training at the General Staff College in Istanbul. Living in the imperial capital for the first time, Kemal immersed himself in a cosmopolitan world of cafes, bars, brothels, and theatres. These distractions did not keep him from joining a circle of young army officers obsessed with the future of the empire. Their discussions drove home to Kemal that "our country was in a terrible state," as he put it.[7] The iron fist of the aging Abdulhamid II and the empire's clear downward spiral convinced many young officers that the old regime had to go. As in China, the imperial army had modernized faster than any other branch of government. All military officers had to learn French, making them part of a tiny elite of Ottoman officials who understood a European language. The young men pored over French history and political theory, absorbing ideas of

The defeat of Turkish armies, shown here in battle, in World War I hurried the final collapse of the Ottoman Empire.

liberty and revolutionary change. Kemal also read Turkish nationalist intellectuals, including Ziya Gökalp and Namık Kemal. At the risk of his promising career and perhaps even his life, Kemal and a few others began to publish a newspaper calling for radical reforms.

In 1904, spies informed on Kemal and his friends. The sultan's police arrested them, and Kemal spent months in prison. Finally they offered him a deal—rather than executing him they would post him to distant Syria. Thus exiled, Kemal could do little harm, they assumed. As an officer in Syria, Kemal witnessed the Ottoman army suppress a local rebellion. The brutal way his fellow officers treated their Arab subjects shocked him. Perhaps it was true that Turks should rule only themselves and not others.

THE YOUNG TURKS

Kemal managed to get a transfer back to his home town of Salonika, where he once again plunged into revolutionary politics, inviting a group of trusted friends to tear down "this rotten, worn-out adminis-tration . . . to save the motherland."[8] Kemal and the others later joined the underground Committee for Union and Progress (CUP), a major faction in a heterogeneous body of reformers that has gone down in history as the "Young Turks." The CUP demanded that the sultan restore the Constitution of 1876, reconvene parliament, and move for-ward with other urgent reforms. In 1908, the Young Turks at last struck, surrounding the sultan's palace and forcing Adbulhamid II to restore the constitution. The following year, they deposed him in favor of a more pliant Mehmed V.

Before the Young Turks could get very far with their reforms, war intervened. Fighting began in the ethnically fragmented Balkans in 1912, pitting the Ottoman army against nationalists in Serbia and Montenegro. Muslims and Christians had lived side by side in these regions for centuries, always aware of their differences but for the most part in peace. As the Christian nationalists came to power, they attacked Turkish civilians, killing thousands and sending many more streaming back toward Anatolia. It came as a crushing blow to Ottoman morale when the independence fighters won.

The Balkan Wars set the stage for the assassination of Austria's Archduke Ferdinand, the event that unleashed a global conflagration from 1914 to 1918. Ethnic cleansing in the Balkans foreshadowed more terrible events in the Great War. In 1913 the Young Turks overthrew the government they had helped institute, and the next year they took the empire into World War I on the side of Germany. The gamble led to disaster, made worse because of a genocidal policy against Armenian Christians in Anatolia.

The subject of the Armenian genocide remains controversial. At the time and ever since, Turkey has claimed that the Armenians had turned against their own government and were helping Russian troops invading Anatolia from the east. To prevent Armenians from collaborating with the Russians, Armenian populations across Anatolia were marched away from zones of conflict. The official version admits that as many as 800,000 Armenians died due to disease, lack of supplies, and vengeance attacks by Muslims, many of whom were refugees from ethnic cleansing in the Balkans. All Turkish governments from the CUP through the present have denied that the extermination of the Armenians was a deliberate policy deserving the name genocide.

It is certainly true that some Armenians sided with the Russian invaders. But the verdict of eyewitness reports and courageous research by Turkish historians confirms that the Young Turks ordered the systematic killing of the Armenians, who made up 10 percent of Anatolia's population in 1914. The Armenian question matters for more than humanitarian reasons. During the war, the multiethnic Ottoman Empire was collapsing, and a new Turkish nation-state was precipitating out of the fragments. Nationalists believed that to be a Turk meant to be Muslim. In the words of historian Bernard Lewis, "a non-Muslim in Turkey may be called a Turkish citizen, but never a Turk."[9] The CUP thus faced a major dilemma—how would the new Turkish nation deal with its Christian minorities?

MUSTAFA KEMAL, WAR HERO

Mustafa Kemal had ties to the Young Turks but was not among the ruling clique during the war and bore no responsibility for the Armenian genocide. He had, in fact, made a name for himself second to none during the Great War. Assigned to the empire's Western Front as a lieutenant-colonel in charge of an army division, in early 1915 Kemal faced overwhelming odds in a battle for the control of the Dardanelles, the gateway to Istanbul and to Russia's warm-water ports on the Black Sea. The long history of Ottoman military defeat inflated the confidence of the Allies, but Kemal's battle-hardened troops held their ground at Gallipoli and threw back the assault. Like Porfirio Díaz against the French and Menelik II against the Italians, Kemal won a critical victory over a foreign invader and thus became a popular hero. Ottoman officials, however, feared his popularity. "I had thought my rather humble accomplishment would have been appreciated by those running the Ottoman state," Kemal said with a typical blend of humility and arrogance. "I had some opinions about life-and-death problems . . . but I saw that nobody was listening to me."[10]

At the war's end, Kemal understood before most other reformers that it would be impossible to save the empire from dismemberment. The Balkan territories were lost. The Allies had occupied the Arab provinces and promised them independence. With brutal realism, Kemal told his fellow officers that the only hope for the nation was to fight to the death to preserve the Anatolian heartland, letting all the rest go. Indeed, Turks should be glad to be rid of the empire. "Do you know how many human beings perished in order to hold Syria and Iraq, to make it possible to live in Egypt, and to maintain a hold in Africa?" he exclaimed. "The Turkish people cannot undertake such a heavy responsibility."[11]

By the spring of 1919, however, even Anatolia was in danger. Britain controlled strategic points along the Anatolian railroad, as well as the Dardanelles. French armies moved into Anatolia from Syria, reinforced by Italian and Greek armies that landed on the coast. With the nation's survival in doubt, Kemal emerged as the defender of Turkish nationalism, in sharp contrast to the new sultan, Mehmed VI Vahdettin, who in defeat seemed willing to allow the Allies to divide up Anatolia. Realizing that the sultan had discredited himself by accepting the Treaty of Sévres (1920), Kemal ignored Vahdettin's order to surrender and instead rallied a fighting force against the occupiers in the Turkish War of Independence (1920–1923). After expelling an Armenian army from the east and defeating French forces in the south, Kemal took on a much larger Greek force dug in at Izmir. Against formidable odds, he won and the Greeks retreated. Kemal and his allies had freed Anatolia from three occupying armies.

FROM EMPIRE TO REPUBLIC

At the close of the conflict with Greece, the two sides agreed to a transfer of populations. Over a million Greeks left Anatolia, while Greece expelled hundreds of thousands of Turks. From the perspective of

Turkish nationalism, the population transfers completed the process begun with the Armenian genocide. The terrible consequences of the Balkan Wars, World War I, and the War of Independence—ethnic cleansing, genocide, and population transfers—meant that Turkey in 1923 was demographically distinct from the Ottoman Empire of only 20 years earlier. Gone were the empire's largely Christian lands in the Balkans; gone, as well, were the Arabic-speaking regions of the Middle East and North Africa. Even the Anatolian core had changed radically. The Armenian and Greek populations had all but disappeared, while the Muslim majority had been reinforced by the inflow of Balkan refugees. Except for the Kurds of eastern Anatolia, a significant 20 percent of the population who were Muslim but not Turkish, the republic's population now approximated the uniform ethnic, language, and religious group that nationalists of the time—including Adolph Hitler—believed was essential to the creation of a successful nation-state. In the words of historian Kemal Karpat, "the idea of a multinational state based on common citizenship lost its practical importance since the Ottoman state became predominantly inhabited by Muslims."[12]

Kemal's bold defense of Anatolia galvanized Turks and, in a real sense, created a new nation. After decades of failure and defeat, Turks now had reason to be proud. "I have known all nations," Kemal told

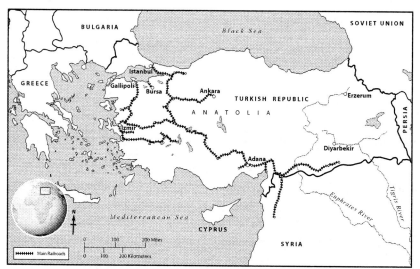

The Turkish republic made its new capital at Ankara, in the Anatolian highlands, far from the ancient seat of Ottoman government in Constantinople, modern-day Istanbul.

his people. "I have studied them on the battlefield . . . when the character of a people is laid naked. I swear to you, my people, that the spiritual strength of our nation transcends that of all the world."[13] By defeating foreign armies that had occupied the length and breadth of Anatolia, Kemal radically changed the political situation on the ground. The British, occupying Istanbul, could not ignore what Kemal had achieved. In 1922 the British and French agreed to negotiate a new treaty with Turkey. Kemal's minimum terms were the full sovereignty of Turkey, total abolition of the Ottoman capitulations, and a fair settlement of the vanished empire's foreign debt. The Treaty of Lausanne (1923) met these demands, recognizing a new Turkish nation.

During the War of Independence, Kemal had stayed out of Istanbul to avoid capture by the British. To the cosmopolitan Turks living in the capital, Kemal was "exiled" to the country's rural interior. Astute as always, Kemal saw that building a base among the peasants of Anatolia was the key to his ambitions. He made his base in Ankara, a sleepy, backward town on the windswept plains of central Anatolia. An American visitor found little to like in Ankara, "where running water is almost unknown, where open drains run down the streets, where roads are bad, buildings are small and dingy . . . where communications are scarce and irregular, where there are few lights in the streets and scarcely any life after dark."[14] This was the "real" Turkey, however, and Kemal embraced it.

In 1920, a new parliament called the Grand National Assembly moved to Ankara from Istanbul. With Kemal's successive victories, the nationalist government in Ankara grew stronger. In 1922, seizing the moment at which the sultan's power was at low ebb, Kemal called on the assembly to abolish the sultanate. Then, on October 29, 1923, the assembly declared Turkey a republic and unanimously elected Mustafa Kemal the new nation's first president. The Ottoman Empire was gone, succeeded by a far smaller and more homogeneous Turkish republic.

A REVOLUTIONARY REPUBLIC

The people of Turkey had lived through two decades of war, turmoil, and death. Most admired their new president, but few could have imagined the rapid, radical changes that Kemal would undertake as president. Observers at the time and since have called Kemal's program a "revolution from above," a century of evolution compressed into a few years.

Kemal could not have accomplished this "revolution" without finely honed political skills. During the War of Independence, he courted the ulema to get their blessing for the creation of a republic—which in short order took away their control of schools and courts. Kemal's government in Ankara appealed to devout Muslims by banning the sale of alcohol and thus "putting teeth into the Koran," as one Westerner said.[15] The ban was lifted soon after the republic was declared in 1923. He also promised the Kurds that the republic would recognize their distinct language and culture and give them some control over their territory in eastern Anatolia. He did not do so, however, and after a Kurdish rebellion in 1925, the republic brutally repressed the Kurds, even banning use of the Kurdish language.

THE FIRST WAVE

When the national assembly had abolished the sultanate, it preserved the sultan's religious role as caliph. But that, it turned out, was a temporary maneuver. Since the caliph theoretically represented all Sunni Muslims, Kemal saw the institution as a remnant of the empire with its world-spanning ambitions and thus contrary to his goal of a strictly Turkish nation. "The caliphate has sucked us white for centuries," he declared. "It is time that Turkey looks to herself . . . [and] rids herself of the leadership of Islam."[16] In 1924, Kemal went before the Grand National Assembly, in which his supporters held a majority, and urged it to eliminate the caliphate. On March 3, they did. The last members of the ancient Ottoman dynasty boarded ship and sailed into exile.

Abolishing the caliphate did more than end Turkey's pretension to be the international defender of Islam. It also eliminated a likely enemy of Kemal's plan to modernize Turkey. From the failures of ill-fated reformers like Selim III, Kemal concluded that he had to destroy the structures that supported the old regime. He struck first at the sultan, the political pillar of the reactionaries, then at the caliph, their religious prop.

Turkey was now a republic, and in a republic the people ruled, or so Kemal said. In the face of likely opposition to his reforms, however, Kemal did not allow too much democracy. Though he had been freely elected, Kemal asked the assembly for extraordinary powers. In March 1925 it approved the Maintenance of Order Act, which allowed the president to close newspapers critical of the government and to arrest political opponents. The government created special "independence tribunals" to try enemies of the state. The tribunals eventually sentenced over 600 people to death. In a moment of candor, Kemal admitted that "it was the people that I was afraid of."[17]

In the meantime Kemal moved ahead with steps to secularize Turkey by separating religion from government as much as possible. To that end, he urged the national assembly to end the ulema's control of the schools and courts. In 1924, all schools in the republic passed under control of the education ministry. The medreses, or religious schools, closed, except for a few programs to train *mullahs*, or Muslim clerics. The change was not cosmetic, since Kemal believed that new schools would be the factories that produce forward-looking Turks. The new ministry of education reached out to leading experts in teaching. John Dewey, an educational innovator at Columbia University, traveled to Turkey in 1924 and helped design a modern grade-school curriculum. The government built new universities as well. When Adolph Hitler purged Jewish professors from Germany's universities in the 1930s, Turkey welcomed them, giving faculty posts to more than 170 refugees, including several world-renowned scientists and scholars—an echo of Ottoman policy in 1492, when Bayezid II had welcomed Jewish refugees expelled from Spain by Ferdinand and Isabela.

The secularization campaign continued in 1926 when the assembly replaced the Ottoman legal system by adopting the Swiss civil code, the German commercial code, and the Italian penal code. The republic's minister of justice explained that Turkey was choosing "the best that Western civilization has to offer."[18] The new legal system ended the control of religious courts over family matters. Women now had the same rights as men in divorce proceedings, and civil marriage replaced religious weddings. Polygamy, which had become rare but was allowed under religious law, became illegal.

THE NEW WOMAN

Many of the republic's early reforms affected women, and Western newspapers celebrated the "new women" of Turkey who competed in beauty contests, smoked in public, and danced to American jazz. Women's rights was a serious issue, however. Turkey's rapidly expanding school system welcomed girls, and by 1934 newspapers reported that "today the schools and universities are full of girls eager to learn."[19] Women who had not dared to work alongside men now routinely took jobs in stores and offices. A surprising number of women entered the law and medicine. In 1934 the national assembly gave Turkish women the right to vote, years before France and Italy did so. The following year 17 women won election to the national assembly. Women in Kemal's republic became outspoken advocates for women's rights in the Middle East and worldwide.

The social changes that Western newspapers loved to report on were real enough, at least for middle-class women living in cities. Rose Lee, a journalist who visited the country in 1926, reported that a Turkish woman "may dress as suits her fancy. She may go where she pleases. She may dance and drink and flirt discreetly, or she may devote herself to serious achievement."[20] Supporting new rights for women was a political calculation by Kemal and the reformers, who believed that "emancipated" women would naturally support the new government. Many urban, educated Turkish men also favored the broad new freedoms for women. Still, Kemal could take personal credit for pushing through the new laws. Long before coming to power he had noted in his diary: "Let's be courageous in the matter of women. Let's forget fear."[21] When a Turkish woman won the Miss World pageant in Belgium in 1932, she wired Kemal: "My success is the result of the ideas inspired by you in the women of our country."[22]

MODERNIZING THE MIND

Kemal's first wave of reforms took aim at institutions—the sultanate and the caliphate, schools, and courts—that propped up Turkey's old way of life. The next set of changes cut deeper, seeking to root out and replace aspects of personal identity. Kemal's goal was to create new Turks to people the new republic.

Clothing had long been an important badge of Turkish identity. In Ottoman times, *sumptuary laws* determined the dress of each identifiable group. Greeks, Armenians, and Jews by law wore clothes that set them apart from Muslims. Muslim men, again by law, wore the fez, a distinctive brimless hat. The fez had been a modernizing reform in the 1820s, when it replaced the then-traditional turban. By the 1920s, however, the fez had become a stereotype. In Western newspapers, political cartoons universally pictured Turks as fez-wearing exotics. The fez, Kemal said, "sat on the heads of our nation as an emblem of ignorance, negligence, fanaticism, and hatred of progress and civilization."[23] It had to go.

Although headwear reform may seem trivial, it became a serious— even lethal—issue between modernizers and traditionalists. Muslims had long associated the wearing of brimmed hats with Christian Europe. Indeed, in Turkish the phrase "to put on a hat" meant to betray Islam.[24] Knowing that Turks would not easily give up the fez, Kemal traveled to a small town known for its conservatism to announce the new policy. When the president appeared in a white suit, open-neck shirt, and a Panama hat, the local people stood speechless. Undaunted, Kemal pushed through the "Law Concerning the Wearing of the Hat" in November 1925. Any man wearing the fez after that date was liable to arrest. Anti-hat rebellions flared up across Turkey's rural, eastern provinces. When thousands of protesters gathered in Erzurum, police fired into the crowd, killing 23 people. In Kayseri, 20 leaders of the anti-hat movement were arrested, tried, and executed. Clothing reform was no laughing matter.

REFORMING THE LANGUAGE

Language was another target of Kemal's reforms. For 1,000 years, Turkish had been written in Arabic letters. The fit between the spoken and written language was not good, however. Turkish has eight distinct vowel sounds, whereas written Arabic is consonant based, using accents to indicate vowels. As a result, spoken and written Turkish had diverged, making it difficult to learn to read and write. "Educated Turks . . . spend all their lives learning Turkish," one expert said, "while the mass of the people die without knowing much about it."[25] Indeed, more than 80 percent of Turkey's population was unable to read and write in the mid-1920s.

Determined to reduce illiteracy, Kemal asked Turkish linguists to devise a new alphabet using European letters. In the summer of 1928, the president himself unveiled the curious new alphabet in an open-air seminar in downtown Istanbul. The new letters, he said, would "rescue our tongue from characters which starved our thoughts." Government radio broadcasts told the public that "Arabic characters are unfitted for the needs of expression in modern civilization."[26] The new alphabet was perfectly phonetic—each letter had just one sound. The reformers assumed, correctly, that it would be far easier for the illiterate majority to learn to read and write the new language. Illiteracy declined sharply in the 1930s. The newly literate, of course, could not read anything written in the old Arabic script, effectively cutting them off from 700 years of Ottoman culture. That was precisely what Kemal wanted.

Mustafa Kemal personally introduced many of the reforms he favored for the Turkish republic. Here, he demonstrates the new alphabet that replaced the Arabic letters used in Ottoman script. "You must entirely forget the old orthography," Kemal told one crowd. (*Turkish Cultural Office*)

"TURKIFICATION" OR WESTERNIZATION?

Modernity was a Western invention, so to be modern Turkey had to become, in some ways, more Western. But that was not the whole story. What Kemal wanted was a modern Turkey, not a Turkey drained of its culture. Westerners paid a great deal of attention when Turkey borrowed from the West—for example, when Kemal made Sunday rather than Friday the official day of rest and adopted the Western calendar.

They often ignored the fierce nationalism that underlay other initiatives, such as the language reform campaign launched in the early 1930s.

Over the centuries Turks had adopted many terms from the rich vocabularies of Arabic and Persian. In 1932 Kemal convened the Turkish Language Society to purge Turkish of these foreign words. The society went to work finding "pure" Turkish substitutes for the loanwords. Every week newspapers published lists of now-forbidden words and their Turkish replacements. The society also invented new words from Turkish roots. Newspaper and book publishers had to switch to the "purified" language, but ordinary people went on using the words they knew best without worrying about where they came from. Eventually Turkish linguists hit on a clever if unscientific strategy. They declared that the Arabic and Persian words in common usage actually derived from an ancient Turkish "sun language" and thus did not need to be replaced. Some scholars raised their eyebrows, but Turkey had found a way to nationalize the foreign words.

Another reform involved the introduction of family names. At the time, Turks used only first names, identifying themselves by the town they were from or with an honorific title like Bey or Efendi. In 1934 the republic did away with titles and ordered every Turkish family to choose a last name. In keeping with the goal of Turkification, the government forbade the adoption of last names based on Arabic, Persian, or other foreign words. Like the rest of his people, Mustafa Kemal also had to choose a last name. To recognize the remarkable changes he had wrought in only a decade, the national assembly honored him with the last name Atatürk, meaning "Father of the Turks."

FAILED OPPOSITION

Kemal's reforms had support from many but not all Turks. Some liberals complained that his top-down style of imposing reform was undemocratic. More numerous were those who objected on religious grounds. A Western reporter in remote eastern Turkey found that "a large part of the population are dissatisfied with the principal changes made by the Republicans and . . . dissent from the fundamental Republican doctrine that religion should be separated from politics."[27]

As early as 1924, Kemal's opponents organized the Progressive Republican Party to offer voters an alternative to the president's Popular Party. Only three months after the new party was launched, however,

Kemal used the Law on Maintenance of Order to close it down. Police arrested party leaders, and a number of prominent figures, including some old friends of the president, were executed.

After the repression of the Kurdish rebellion, the anti-hat demonstrations, and the Progressive Republican Party, most Turks understood that if they opposed Kemal they did so at peril of their lives. Turkey became a single-party state, and Kemal was reelected by the national assembly every four years until his death.

MODERNIZING THE ECONOMY

The Ottoman Empire had been even weaker economically than it was militarily. As Kemal put it, "Turkey has often produced conquerors, but never economists."[28] A 1915 survey showed that the empire had little modern industry—there were only 284 factories with more than 50 employees. (By contrast, the state of North Carolina in 1909 had over 200 cotton mills with over 50 employees—and that was just one of many large industries found throughout the United States.) Moreover, foreigners and non-Muslims controlled 85 percent of the existing industries.

Naturally Kemal and his fellow nationalists planned to modernize the republic's economy. Despite a critical lack of funds, they spent hundreds of millions of dollars constructing railroads to open up Anatolia's interior. Before the railways, observers noted, "surplus grain and other crops either rotted in the fields or were transported in ox-carts." Now these products reached seaports quickly and cheaply for sale in Turkish cities or abroad.[29] The government also used an agricultural bank to provide peasants with credit at far lower rates than the exorbitant loans offered by local merchants.

When the Great Depression began in 1929, private investment and trade plummeted worldwide. In response, Kemal made his government the agent of economic change, a policy he called *statism*. Kemal took inspiration from the rapid industrialization of the Soviet Union, where Stalin had introduced "five-year plans" to build heavy industries. Turkey's first five-year plan drew on existing strengths in agriculture to create processing plants for sugar, tobacco, and cotton. At the same time, the government funded the building of iron and steel works and chemical plants. To launch these modern industries, Turkey still needed foreign expertise and technology, but the new government kept close control of them, owning many of the new

Since his death in 1938, Atatürk has remained the dominant symbol of the Turkish republic. On a visit to Turkey in April 2009, President Barack Obama declared that "the greatest monument to Atatürk's life is. . . . Turkey's strong, vibrant, secular democracy."

factories outright. "Today there is no question of foreign concessions," a Western reporter noted.[30]

When the republic celebrated its first decade in 1933, Turkey had transformed itself dramatically. The new capital at Ankara was a potent symbol of Turkey's leap toward modernity. No longer a village whose residents tethered their donkeys outside government offices, Ankara was now a city of over 100,000 people boasting "ultra-modernist" architecture with "broad avenues . . . sleek new taxi-cabs . . . [and] banks and stores illuminated at night by red and blue neon lights."[31]

LEGACY OF REFORM

"It is necessary to proceed by stages in imposing changes," Kemal had declared, "to prepare the feeling and spirit of the nation."[32] But for many Turks the changes made by the republic hardly seemed gradual. "Sometimes I stop and wonder," one Turkish woman admitted, "if everything I am doing is not a dream."[33] Westerners wondered how long the "dream" would continue. "Have the changes and reforms," a London reporter asked, "been too many, too rapid, and too radical to be permanent?"[34]

In the 1920s and 1930s critics in Europe and the United States often compared Kemal to the Bolsheviks in Russia and Italy's fascist leader Benito Mussolini. He and his fellow radicals "are building a social order only less radical than that of Soviet Russia," the *New York Times* noted in 1936.[35] Indeed, although the Russian and Ottoman empires had been historic enemies, Kemal's Turkey built warm relations with the Soviet Union. Stalin even provided money and advisors for Turkey's five-year plans.

Unlike the Communists, however, Mustafa Kemal was not an ideologue, meaning the fanatic follower of a particular doctrine. He was a pragmatist, and the reforms he pressed upon the Turkish people had practical goals, above all the destruction of old institutions and the creation of new ones that would over time profoundly change Turkish society. Like the Bolsheviks, he secularized his country, taking political power away from religious leaders. Unlike them, however, Kemal did not outlaw religion and make atheism official policy. He knew his people well and did not challenge their devotion to Islam. Although he personally detested the wearing of the veil, for example, his government tolerated its use by Turkish women.

Kemal's goal was not to create a utopia but rather to catch up with the West. "The Turkish nation has fallen far behind the West," he said as early as 1912. "The main aim should be to lead it to modern civilization."[36] Kemal pursued that goal, ruthlessly at times but without sacrificing Turkish identity and culture. When he fell ill with cirrhosis of the liver in 1937, Turks, as well as foreigners, wondered if his reforms would go to the grave with him. After his death in November 1938, however, most of the changes Atatürk had implemented remained in effect, unlike the institutions created by both fascist and Communist leaders which, in the fullness of time, met with nearly complete repudiation.

SOURCES

■ Mustafa Kemal's Great Speech

Mustafa Kemal, president of Turkey, rose before the Grand National Assembly in 1927 to give his account of the remarkable events the country had lived through since World War I, including the War of Independence, the abolition of the sultanate and caliphate, the repression of the republic's enemies, and the early reforms. Kemal spoke for six hours a day for six days. In Turkish, this marathon oration is called simply *Nutuk*, "The Speech." In print it runs to over 600 pages.

In the excerpts that follow, Kemal explains how he made decisions at critical moments to move forward with the creation of the Turkish republic. As you read, ask yourself why it served Kemal's political goals in 1927 to make the postwar situation seem as bleak as possible and to make the Ottoman Empire look terminally weak. According to Kemal, did most Turks believe the nation could survive without a sultan or a caliph? How likely did it seem that Turkey could defeat the allied occupiers at the war's end?

The group of Powers which included the Ottoman Government had been defeated in the Great War. The Ottoman Army had been crushed on every front. An armistice had been signed under severe conditions. The prolongation of the Great War had left the people exhausted and impoverished. . . .

Morally and materially, the enemy Powers were openly attacking the Ottoman Empire and the country itself. They were determined to disintegrate and annihilate both. The Padishah[37] Caliph[38] had one sole anxiety namely, to save his own life . . . Without being aware of it, the nation had no longer any one to lead it, but lived in darkness and uncertainty, waiting to see what would happen. . . .

The Army existed merely in name. The commanders and other officers were still suffering from the exhaustion resulting from the war. Their hearts were bleeding on account of the threatened dismemberment of their country. Standing on the brink of the dark abyss which yawned before their eyes, they racked their brains to discover a way out of the danger.

Source: Speech delivered by Ghazi Mustapha Kemal, President of the Turkish Republic, October 1927 (Leipzig: K. F. Koehler, 1929), available at http://www.archive.org/stream/speechdeliveredg010347mbp/speechdeliveredg010347mbp_djvu.txt.

Here I must add and explain a very important point, the Nation and the Army had no suspicion at all of the Padishah-Caliph's treachery. On the contrary, on account of the close connection between religion and tradition handed down for centuries, they remained loyal to the throne and its occupant. . . . That the country could possibly be saved without a Caliph and without a Padishah was an idea too impossible for them to comprehend. And woe to those who ventured to think otherwise! They would immediately have been looked down upon as men without faith and without patriotism and as such would have been scorned.

. . . . In seeking how to save the situation it was considered to be specially important to avoid irritating the Great Powers England, France and Italy. The idea that it was impossible to fight even one of these Powers had taken root in the mind of nearly everybody. Consequently, to think of doing so and thus bring on another war after the Ottoman Empire, all-powerful Germany and Austria-Hungary together had been defeated and crushed would have been looked upon as sheer madness. . . .

In reality, the foundations of the Ottoman Empire were themselves shattered at that time. . . . All the Ottoman districts were practically dismembered. Only one important part of the country . . . still remained, and it was now suggested also to divide this.

Such expressions as: the Ottoman Empire, Independence, Padishah-Caliph, Government all of them were mere meaningless words.

Therefore, whose existence was it essential to save? and with whose help? and how? But how could these questions be solved at such a time as this?

The Idea of the Republic

As Kemal explains below, he realized the need to create a new Turkish state out of the ruins of the Ottoman Empire. What institutions, according to Kemal, did he and his supporters have to fight against? Kemal admits that "we never disclosed the views we held" about the future of the nation. Why would that be the case? What does that policy suggest about Kemal's future commitment to democracy? How much credit does Kemal take personally for leading the nation toward its rebirth?

In these circumstances, one resolution alone was possible, namely, to create a New Turkish State, the sovereignty and independence of which would be unreservedly recognised by the whole world.

This was the resolution we adopted before we left Constantinople and which we began to put into execution immediately we set foot on Anatolian soil[39]. . . .

As you see, in order to carry out our resolution . . . it was imperative that questions should be brought forward that could not be discussed in public without giving rise to serious dissentions.

We were compelled to rebel against the Ottoman Government, against the Padishah, against the Caliph of all the Mohammedans,[40] and we had to bring the whole nation and the army into a state of rebellion. . . .

As the national struggle, carried on for the sole purpose of delivering the country from foreign invasion, developed and was crowned with success. . . . we never disclosed the views we held. If we had done so we would have been looked upon as dreamers and illusionists. If we had offered explanations we might from the outset have alienated those who, discouraged by the possibilities arising from dangers that threatened from abroad, were fearful of eventual revolutionary changes which would be contrary to their tradition, their way of thinking and their psychology. The only practical and safe road to success lay in making each step perfectly understood at the right time. This was the way to ensure the development and restoration of the nation. . . .

It was incumbent upon me to develop our entire social organisation, step by step, until it corresponded to the great capability of progress which I perceived in the soul and in the future of the nation and which I kept to myself in my own consciousness as a national secret. . . .

■ Abolishing the Sultanate

When the national assembly debated abolishing the sultanate in 1922, Kemal played the leading role in urging this momentous step. In his statement before the assembly, how does Kemal sweep aside the delegates' worries about their authority to eliminate the sultanate? Do Kemal's views about sovereignty suggest that he will be a powerful voice in favor of democracy?

I made some statements [in the Grand National Assembly] . . . to prove the necessity for the abolition of the Sultanate. . . .

Speaking of the history of Islam and of Turkey, based on historical facts, I showed that the Caliphate and the Sultanate could be separated from one another and that the Grand National Assembly could possess the national sovereignty. . . .

Standing on the bench in front of me, I made this statement in a loud voice: "Gentlemen," I declared, "neither the sovereignty nor the right to govern can be transferred by one person to anybody else by an academic debate. Sovereignty is acquired by force, by power and by violence. It was by violence that the sons of Osman[41] acquired the power to rule over the Turkish nation and to maintain their rule for more than six centuries. It is now the nation that revolts against these usurpers, puts them in their right place and actually carries on their sovereignty. This is an actual fact. It is no longer a question of knowing whether we want to leave this sovereignty in the hands of the nation or not. It is simply a question of stating . . . an accomplished fact and which must be accepted unconditionally as such. And this must be done at any price. If those who are assembled here, the Assembly and everybody else would find this quite natural, it would be very appropriate from my point of view. Conversely, the reality will nevertheless be manifested in the necessary form, but in that event it is possible that some heads will be cut off. . . .

■ Suppressing the Republic's Enemies

After the declaration of the republic on October 29, 1923, Kemal became the new nation's first president. Faced with opposition in some parts of the country, Kemal asked the national assembly to pass the *Law for the Maintenance of Order,* which allowed him to close newspapers and arrest opponents. How does Kemal defend the use of these undemocratic powers? How do you think the failed plan to assassinate Kemal made him feel about handling opposition to the new government?

The Government . . . caused the law regarding the maintenance of order to be proclaimed, and the Independence Courts to take action. For a considerable time they kept eight or nine divisions of the army at war strength for the suppression of disorders, and put an end to the injurious organisation which bore the name "Republican Progressive Party."

The result was, of course, the success of the Republic. The insurgents were destroyed. But the enemies of the Republic did not consider this defeat the last phase of the controversy. In an unworthy manner they played their last card which took the form of the Smyrna attack.[42] The avenging hand of Republican justice again mastered the army of conspirators and saved the Republic.

Honourable Gentlemen, when, in consequence of serious necessity we became convinced . . . that it would be useful for the Government to take extraordinary measures, there were people who . . . thought that we were making use of the law for the Maintenance of Order and the Courts of Independence as tools of dictatorship or despotism.

There is no doubt that time and events will show to those who dissem- inated this opinion how mistaken they were, and put them to shame.

We never used the exceptional measures, which all the same were legal, to set ourselves in any way above the law.

On the contrary, we applied them to restore peace and quiet in the country. We made use of them to insure the existence and indepen- dence of the country. We made use of them with the object of contribut- ing to the social development of the nation. . . .

■ Early Reforms

At the end of the *Great Speech*, Kemal turned briefly to the major reforms that had been instituted in the republic's first few years. According to Kemal, would it have been possible to ban the wearing of the fez without the law for the Maintenance of Order? Throughout this excerpt, what attitude does he convey regarding Turkey's tradi- tional culture and, in particular, Islam?

It was necessary to abolish the fez, which sat on our heads as a sign of ignorance, of fanaticism, of hatred to progress and civilisation, and to adopt in its place the hat, the customary head-dress of the whole civilised world, thus showing, among other things, that no difference existed in the manner of thought between the Turkish nation and the whole family of civilised mankind. We did that while the law for the Maintenance of Order was still in force. If it had not been in force we should have done so all the same; but one can say with complete truth that the existence of this law made the thing much easier for us. As a matter of fact the application of the law for the Maintenance of Order prevented the morale of the nation being poisoned . . . by reactionaries. . . .

Gentlemen, while the law regarding the Maintenance of Order was in force there took place also the closing of the Tekkes,[43] of the con- vents, and of the mausoleums,[44] as well as the abolition of all sects and all kinds of titles such as Sheikh,[45] Dervish[46] . . . Occultist, Magician, Mausoleum Guard, etc.

One will be able to imagine how necessary the carrying through of these measures was, in order to prove that our nation as a whole was no primitive nation, filled with superstitions and prejudices.

Could a civilised nation tolerate a mass of people who let themselves be led by the nose by a herd of Sheikhs . . . Babas[47] and Emirs;[48] who entrusted their destiny and their lives to magicians, dice-throwers and amulet sellers? Ought one to conserve in the Turkish State, in the Turkish

Republic, elements and institutions such as those which had for centuries given the nation the appearance of being other than it really was?

.... If we made use of the law for the Maintenance of Order in this manner, it was in order to avoid such a historic error; to show the nation's brow pure and luminous, as it is; to prove that our people think neither in a fanatical nor a reactionary manner.

Gentlemen, at the same time the new laws were worked out and decreed which promise the most fruitful results for the nation on the social and economic plane, and in general in all the forms of the expression of human activity ... the Citizens Law-book, which ensures the liberty of women and stabilises the existence of the family.

Accordingly we made use of all circumstances only from one point of view, which consisted therein: to raise the nation on to that step on which it is justified in standing in the civilised world, to stabilise the Turkish Republic more and more on steadfast foundations ... and in addition to destroy the spirit of despotism forever....

Gentlemen, I have taken trouble to show, in these accounts, how a great people ... reconquered its independence; how it created a national and modern State founded on the latest results of science....

This holy treasure I lay in the hands of the youth of Turkey.

NOTES

1. "Says America Has Balance of Power," *New York Times*, December 9, 1921, p. 2.
2. "Kemal Is Turkey's Peter the Great," *New York Times*, August 8, 1926, p. SM7.
3. Eliot Grinnell Mears, ed., *Modern Turkey* (New York: Macmillan, 1924), p. 354.
4. Kemal H. Karpat, "The Transformation of the Ottoman State, 1789–1908," *International Journal of Middle East Studies* 3: 3 (July, 1972), p. 243.
5. İlhan Akşit, ed., *Mustafa Kemal Atatürk* (Istanbul: Akşit Kültür Turizm Ltd., 1998), p. 11.
6. Ibid., pp. 13–14.
7. Ibid., p. 16.
8. Ibid., p. 23.
9. Bernard Lewis, *The Emergence of Modern Turkey* (New York: Oxford University, 1961), p. 15.
10. Akşit, *Atatürk*, p. 48.
11. Eleanor Bigsbee, *The New Turks: Pioneers of the Republic, 1920–1950* (Philadelphia: University of Pennsylvania, 1951), p. 19.
12. Karpat, "Transformation," p. 272.
13. "Mustafa Kemal as a Tamerlane Born Out of His Time," *New York Times*, March 5, 1933, p. BR3.
14. "Modernization of Turkey," *New York Times*, March 1, 1925, p. BR12.
15. "Struggle Over Anatolia," *New York Times*, December 18, 1921, p. 87.

16. "Mustafa Kemal as a Tamerlane," *New York Times*, March 5, 1933, p. BR3.

17. Ellen Kay Trimberger, *Revolution from Above* (New Brunswick, NJ: Transaction, 1978), p. 35.

18. "Minister of Justice Tells of New Turkey," *New York Times*, October 26, 1926, p. 8.

19. "Women in Turkey Make Big Advance," *New York Times*, December 16, 1934, p. E3.

20. "Turkey's 'Forgotten' Women Are Astir," *New York Times*, June 20, 1926, p. SM4.

21. Andrew Mango, *Atatürk: The Biography of the Founder of Modern Turkey* (New York: Woodstock Press, 2002), p. 176.

22. "Feminism in Turkey," *Times* (London), November 12, 1932, p. 11.

23. Lewis, *Emergence of Modern Turkey*, p. 263.

24. Houchang Chehabi, "Dress Codes for Men in Turkey and Iran," in Touraj Atabaki and Erik J. Zürcher, eds., *Men of Order: Authoritarian Modernization Under Atatürk and Reza Shah* (New York: I.B. Tauris, 2004), p. 212.

25. "New Turkish Alphabet," *Times* (London), August 28, 1928, p. 11.

26. "Mustapha Kemal and New Alphabet," *Times* (London), August 11, 1928, p. 10; "Turkey Expects a Literature to Flower from New Alphabet," *New York Times*, November 18, 1928, p. 7.

27. "The Troubles of Turkey," *Times* (London), February 25, 1925, p. 15.

28. "Mustapha Kemal," *Times* (London), January 18, 1923, p. 9.

29. "In Turkey the Modern Age Marches On," *New York Times*, May 29, 1932, p. SM12.

30. "New Turkey Keeps to Her Course," *New York Times*, November 27, 1938, p. 138.

31. "The City that Reveals the New Turkey," *New York Times*, March 8, 1936, p. SM11.

32. Trimberger, *Revolution from Above*, p. 25.

33. "Turkey's 'Forgotten' Women," *New York Times*, June 20, 1926, p. SM4.

34. "Reform in Turkey: Some Causes for Anxiety," *Times* (London), August 11, 1930, p. 9.

35. "The City that Reveals the New Turkey," *New York Times*, March 8, 1936, p. SM11.

36. Mango, *Atatürk*, p. 95.

37. A Persian title roughly translated as "great king" or "emperor." The reference is to the Ottoman sultan.

38. An Arabic term meaning "deputy [of the Prophet]," or leader of the entire Islamic community.

39. In 1919.

40. An archaic European term for Muslims.

41. Osman I (d. 1324?) had founded the Ottoman dynasty by declaring his independence from the Seljuk Turks around 1300, and his descendants created the Ottoman Empire.

42. An attempt to assassinate Mustafa Kemal in 1926.

43. Houses where Sufi brethren, such as the Mevlavi Brothers, the so-called Whirling Dervishes, gathered.

44. The graves of Sufi saints that had become places of pilgrimage.

45. An Arabic title of respect meaning "elder," which is accorded to a person of authority.

46. A Persian title that normally was accorded to mendicant, or begging, ascetics— that is, Sufi saints.

47. Turkish, meaning "fathers." Baba was a term of respect accorded religious leaders.

48. Arabic for "commanders" or "governors."

Epilogue: Making Connections
The Roads to Modernity

This book has emphasized how the Industrial Revolution in the West, and the unprecedented power that modern industry gave to a handful of nations, reverberated across the periphery in the 19th and 20th centuries. The emergence of a core of powerful, dynamic industrial nations changed history, making the gradual evolution of human societies that had been normal before 1800 seem like stagnation. After witnessing the spectacular increase in U.S. power in the late 1800s, the Puerto Rican intellectual Eugenio Maria de Hostos warned the people of the Caribbean that industrial civilization would absorb them "brutally" unless they changed. "The verdict of the times is final," Hostos concluded: "Civilization or death."[1]

It is easy, looking back from the 21st century, to assume that the ascent of the West was natural and inevitable, based primarily on Western breakthroughs in productivity, technology, and science. In reality, military might backed up Western economic power at all times: Recall the U.S. and French invasions of Mexico, Italy's attack on Ethiopia, and the Great Power pressure on China and occupation of Turkey. We could add, to verify the point made by Hostos above, the American military occupations of Cuba, Puerto Rico, Haiti, and the Dominican Republic after 1898. In other words, sudden assault by *armed* forces rather than gradual conquest by *market* forces gave urgency to defensive modernization in the periphery.

The first order of business for modernizers, then, was to protect their nations from military threats from the West. Standing up to the power of the West, they knew, demanded drastic changes in their largely premodern societies. To that end, modernizers pursued "great leaps forward," to use the term that Mao Zedong made notorious in the late 1950s. The "leaps" would accelerate history, using the power of the state to quickly reach modernizing goals that otherwise might take decades or even centuries to achieve. "We are determined not to follow evolutionary change," Sun Yatsen told his followers, "but insist upon artificial change with its faster progress." Mao Zedong was even more impatient with the slow pace of China's development. "10,000 years are too long" he declared in 1963. "Seize the day, seize the hour."[2]

CENTRALIZATION

One common goal of modernizers was centralization of state power. All sought to strengthen the central government, reduce the autonomy of local leaders, create a disciplined national army, and hammer distinct regions into a unified nation. This process, called nation building, was not pretty, and modernizers did not shy away from using violence against their own people to accomplish it. Even the bookish Sun Yatsen eventually became a warlord.

Think about each of the four leaders explored in this book. What did each do to strengthen the central government? Can you see a general pattern in their efforts to build powerful states? Against which groups did each deploy violence? What justified the pursuit of national unity at all cost? Consider how modernizers treated ethnic or religious minorities—indigenous people in Mexico, Armenians and Greeks in Turkey, non-Christians in Ethiopia. What does that treatment tell us about the construction of a modern nation-state?

INFRASTRUCTURE AND INDUSTRY

As modernizers saw it, constructing a powerful nation meant building infrastructure and promoting industry. The problem in all parts of the global periphery was that Europeans or Americans usually controlled the modern sectors of the economy. Nationalists wanted to reduce the role of foreigners in their economies but realized they could not do without capital and technology from abroad. That circle was hard to square.

In the dreams of modernizers, railroads loomed large. These capital-intensive projects promised to make export agriculture profitable, knit nations together, and allow troops to quickly quell uprisings. Yet throughout the periphery, foreigners financed and engineered rail lines, as the stock certificate on this book's cover reminds us. How did the participation of foreign investors make railroads controversial in Mexico, Ethiopia, and China? Did any modernizer find ways to attract foreign investment without weakening national sovereignty? Compare the economic development strategies of Porfirio Díaz and Mustafa Kemal. What did Kemal understand about the political implications of foreign investment that Díaz did not? Is *statism* an accurate term to describe the approach to economic development in all four countries?

SECULARIZATION

Modernizers often confronted religious leaders, if not religion itself, as an obstacle to rapid change. Menelik II criticized the conservatism of Ethiopia's Christian priests and even slowed the pace of economic change to avoid alarming them. On the other hand, the emperor clearly understood that representing himself as ruler of a Christian people strengthened his hand in dealings with Europe. (See Menelik's letter at the end of Chapter 2.) Mustafa Kemal saw the worldly power of Muslim clergy as an impediment to progress and dared to dismantle religious control of schools and law courts. (See the excerpt from Kemal's Great Speech at the end of Chapter 4.) And while Sun Yatsen did not directly challenge the complex polytheism of his people, the fact that he became and remained a Christian was, in its own way, a negative judgment on their religious beliefs. Mexico was exceptional, since Porfirio Díaz purposely avoided open conflict with the Catholic Church, focusing instead on economic change. In none of our cases did the religious establishment rally to the side of modernization. What might explain why that pattern held across such very different societies?

NATIONAL IDENTITY

Modernizing leaders also constructed a sense of national identity among their people. Mustafa Kemal did so most explicitly, employing language and history to reinforce Turkishness at the expense of cosmopolitan Ottomanism. Menelik II welded Ethiopians together as a single people through the struggle against Italian imperialism. Sun united the Chinese people by insisting on the foreignness of the Manchus. All believed that a strong sense of national identity was crucial to building a modern nation-state.

Once again, Mexico was the great exception. There, Díaz unintentionally fostered a sense of Mexican identity through his openness to foreigners, Americans in particular. The revolution that forced Díaz to flee in 1911 expressed a powerful new nationalism that, at least officially, embraced Mexico's indigenous heritage. By the 1920s, Mexican artists such as Diego Rivera and José David Alfaro Siqueiros blended European techniques with Aztec and Mayan imagery. The post-revolutionary government welcomed their vision of a mixed-race Mexico and commissioned them to create huge murals in public buildings, where all Mexicans could see them.

It is too simple, however, to see Díaz as a traitor to his people and the other leaders as legitimate nationalists. All modernizers celebrated "the people," even as they took steps to remake them radically. Kemal exalted Turkishness, while stripping away Islamic institutions that most Turks saw as the essence of their identity. Sun Yatsen praised China's ancient culture but worked unceasingly to bring down the empire that had maintained that culture for over 2,000 years; he also promoted fundamental changes in Chinese society. (See Sun's writings at the end of Chapter 3.) Menelik II created a unified Ethiopia by conquering and absorbing non-Christian peoples, thereby permitting only one variety of national identity. Thus, while Díaz was the only modernizer who paid the price for radically remaking his nation, all the modernizers sought to do so.

In short, most nationalist modernizers incarnated a contradiction. As nationalists, they embodied the spirit and traditions of their people, but as modernizers they demanded radical changes in both. To gain power, of course, nationalists could hardly campaign on the platform that time-honored traditions and ways of life had to be discarded. Yet Westerners observed that the rapid changes taking place in "backward" countries, as they called them, meant that tradition had become the enemy of progress. "Young China demands the abolition of the ancient family tradition which has interfered with progress," the *New York Times* noted in 1928, "and Young Turkey has loosed the religious bonds that have kept her back."[3] Modernizers might be hailed as the fathers of their country, but they were strict patriarchs who demanded that their "children" mature rapidly and leave the past behind.

Modernizers were nationalists, but their vision of the future was global. Throughout the periphery, anti-colonial leaders had one foot in their premodern homelands and the other in the fully modernized West. India's first prime minister after independence in 1947, Jawaharlal Nehru, "was essentially a man of the West," a product of an elite British prep school and Cambridge University, and as such a nationalist whose profound love of India "did not extend to its institutions."[4] The Hindu religion "did not attract" Nehru, and he felt real antipathy toward India's ancient caste system.[5] Jomo Kenyatta, who led Kenya's fight for independence against Britain in the 1950s and in 1963 became the new nation's first prime minister, had completed a doctorate in anthropology at the London School of Economics. Kwame Nkrumah, who steered Ghana to independence and became that nation's first president, earned a master's degree at the University of Pennsylvania before doing further graduate work in England. Eric Williams championed nationhood for Trinidad and Tobago after completing his Ph.D. in London. Muhammad Ali Jinnah, the founder of modern Pakistan, was a London-trained lawyer. Even Mohandas Gandhi, the symbol of nonviolent resistance to British rule, who is invariably pictured wearing the traditional *dhoti*, or white loincloth, of India's impoverished peasantry, was a barrister trained in London.

The modernizing nationalists we examined in this book did not graduate from elite Western universities. Like the anti-colonial leaders who did, however, they were urbane and cosmopolitan in comparison with the peasant majorities at home. That gap between ruler and ruled meant that even as modernizers identified themselves with "the people," they did not necessarily trust the poor majority to understand what modernization would entail. "We never disclosed the views we held," Mustafa Kemal admitted about the struggle to create the Turkish republic. "If we had done so we would have been looked upon as dreamers."[6]

DEMOCRACY

The fact that modernizers planned radical changes in how their people lived also explains why they were not deeply dedicated to democracy. Neither Díaz nor Menelik took democracy seriously. Kemal created a republic based on majority rule but outlawed opposition parties and violently repressed any who opposed his reforms. Sun Yatsen made democracy one of his Three Principles of the People but in practice found that political survival had more to do with armies than elections in the Chinese republic he helped create.

The problem was that the changes brought about by modernization were not necessarily popular. "Ancient philosophies have to be scrapped;" a United Nations report on development explained in 1951, "old social institutions have to disintegrate; bonds of caste, creed and race have to burst; and large numbers of persons who cannot keep up with progress have to have their expectations of a comfortable life frustrated."[7] Not surprisingly, then, modernization often faced stiff opposition, from both elites and ordinary people, forcing leaders to choose between progress and democracy. In India, Jawaharlal Nehru pushed policies similar to Kemal's reforms in Turkey, including equal rights for women, universal education, and government support for industry. But since Nehru, unlike Atatürk, respected civil liberties and allowed real democracy, many of the reforms remained a dead letter, passed by India's parliament but never implemented because of strong opposition from traditionalists.

Throwing out old values came at a price. During Kemal's rapid transformation of Turkey, suicide rates, for men in particular, shot up. The republic's leaders worried about the "disintegrating factors in its Westernization," yet there was no way to have rapid cultural change without anxiety and dislocation. Indeed, the Hungarian critic Georg Lukács coined the term "transcendental homelessness" for this sense of unease and displacement, which he insisted was the essence of the modern condition.[8]

SOCIAL ENGINEERING

The "leaps forward" proposed by modernizers shared in a larger 20th-century trend in which ruling elites tried to remake whole societies. "The political history of the 20th century," conservative columnist David Brooks noted in February 2009, "is the history of social-engineering projects executed by well-intentioned people that began well and ended badly."[9] The observation echoes historian James C. Scott's analysis of ruling groups who used "state power to bring about huge, utopian changes in people's work habits, living patterns, moral conduct, and worldview."[10] Scott finds that authoritarian governments, convinced that they knew what was best for the people, often imposed plans without taking into account local realities. As a result, the plans usually failed, sometimes catastrophically.

Brazil in the late 1950s provides a relatively benign example of a modernizing elite eager to transform its people. As described by Scott, President Juscelino Kubitschek, who promised Brazilians "fifty years of progress in five years," pushed forward a plan for a new capital city a thousand kilometers inland from Rio and Sao Paolo. Kubitschek commissioned modernist architects to design a city that would be free of crowded streets and neighborhoods. Their grand design for Brasilia, as the new capital was called, intentionally cut residential blocks off from shopping areas and office buildings. The modernists wanted Brasilia to transform the lives of Brazilians—"from their personal habits and household organization to their social lives, leisure, and work."[11] The sidewalk cafés, small parks, and public squares that gave life to other Latin American cities did not exist in Brasilia. The landscape was ultramodern, but sterile. The first residents of the new capital found that they suffered from a sense of dislocation which they called *Brasilite*, or Brasilia-itis. Although growth has changed the city, even today aerial photos show the inhuman scale of Brasilia's modernist design.

A far more tragic experiment in social engineering took place in the Soviet Union from 1928 to 1933. Under the steely command of Josef Stalin, the world's first Communist country launched collectivization, an attempt to make agriculture more productive in order to promote rapid industrialization. Bolsheviks had long admired "American methods of extensive farming utilizing tractors and other agricultural machines," which impressed leaders as for more advanced than the primitive methods employed by Russian peasants. Beginning in 1928 Stalin moved ruthlessly to replace "small peasant holdings with large state and collective farms in all parts of the country irrespective of local or regional conditions."[12] The collective farms, officials said, would be more efficient than small farms, producing more food, releasing labor to work in factories, and generating profits that could subsidize industrial growth. In fact, collectivization backfired catastrophically, resulting in devastating famines that killed at least 10 million people due to starvation or disease caused by malnutrition. Most historians now agree that the disaster resulted directly from the Soviet leadership's "struggle to transform an agrarian empire into an industrial power."[13]

Scott's critique of these failed attempts to impose a new social order clearly has some application to our examples. In each case, modernization was a top-down process, designed without consulting those who were to be "modernized," that caused real

Josef Stalin ruled the Soviet Union with an iron fist from the late 1920s until his death in 1953. Stalin understood that World War II had weakened European control over colonies in Asia and Africa and supported "national liberation movements" against "capitalist imperialism." (*Library of Congress*)

suffering for millions of people. The modernizers of N
Ethiopia, China, and Turkey sought radical changes in "pe
work habits, living patterns, moral conduct, and worldview," just
as Scott says.

Unlike the schemes that Scott describes, however, the leaps
examined in this book were not merely "utopian plans"—that is, pipe
dreams that failed at a huge cost in human life, liberty, and happiness.
Our four modernizers all succeeded, to greater or lesser degrees,
although to do so they resorted to brutal, often lethal, force. Even
Díaz, hounded from his homeland and cursed to this day, left
something positive behind: "Porfirian development policies . . .
bequeathed to twentieth-century Mexico an industrial foundation for
the more aggressive import-substitution policies of the 1940s and
1950s."[14] Menelik succeeded in creating modern Ethiopia and keeping European colonizers at bay. Sun Yatsen laid the political foundation for a modern republic. Although Turks now criticize many of
Kemal's reforms as un- or even anti-Muslim, they remain in place as
fundamental tenets of the Turkish republic. Kemal's five-year economic plans also set Turkey on a path to industrialization that makes
it, even today, the most important manufacturing nation of the
Middle East.

MODERNIZATION AND THE COLD WAR

The tribulations of modernizers before World War II captured the
attention of some Westerners but was not a major issue for the Great
Powers. Nevertheless, events in China and Turkey in the 1920s foreshadowed questions of life and death, war and peace, that would
emerge on the world stage in the postwar period. As we saw, soon
after coming to power, the Bolsheviks were eager to give material
support and "guidance" to revolutionary changes underway in those
neighboring nations. The world's only Communist state presented
the socialist road to modernization as the path of least resistance for
poor, premodern societies. In other words, nearly 25 years before the
Cold War officially began in the ashes of World War II, we find
Communists and capitalists competing for the allegiance of the
world's less-developed nations. "Since the war we have been watching two peoples, you and the Russians," the Turkish feminist Halidé
Edib told a group of Americans in 1928. "You represent democracy

and they represent communism. We want to see how each of the two movements will succeed."[15]

Even after a devastating civil war, Russia seemed to be making rapid progress under Bolshevik leadership. Although part of Russia lay in Europe, most of its vast territory was in Asia, underpopulated and decidedly premodern. The Communist development strategy—using state power to plan and speed up economic growth—was in one way simply a variation on a tactic that modernizers were already using. Modernizing leaders had no qualms about wielding the visible hand of government, rather than the "invisible hand" of the market, to reach their goals—from government-bankrolled railroads in Turkey to the expropriation of Indian lands in Mexico.

In the 1930s, the attraction of the socialist road to development grew stronger. Despite the terrible cost of collectivization, which Soviet leaders did their best to conceal, Communism pointed a new way forward to the colonies and poor nations of the world. The Great Depression paralyzed Western capitalist countries, yet the Soviet Union continued to industrialize rapidly (although at a terrible human cost) under Stalin's five-year plans. The future leader of India, Jawaharlal Nehru, followed events in Russia with passionate interest even during his frequent imprisonments by the British in the 1930s. In his 1935 autobiography, Nehru makes clear why leaders of poor countries and colonies overlooked the lack of political freedom in the Soviet Union, focusing instead on its rapid modernization.

> I watched and studied, as far as I could in jail, the world situation in the grip of the great depression. . . . Much in Soviet Russia I dislike—the ruthless suppression of all contrary opinion, the wholesale regimentation, the unnecessary violence (as I thought) in carrying out various policies. But there was no lack of violence and suppression in the capitalist world. . . .
>
> With all her blunders, Soviet Russia had triumphed over enormous difficulties and taken great strides . . . While the rest of the world was in the grip of the depression and going backward in some ways, in the Soviet country a great new world was being built up before our eyes. . . . In particular, I was impressed by the reports of the great progress made by the backward regions of Central Asia under the Soviet regime. In the balance, therefore, . . . the presence and example of the Soviets was a bright and heartening phenomenon in a dark and dismal world.[16]

The contest between capitalist and Communist modernization grew sharper after World War II, as independence movements challenged European colonial rule across the periphery. In many colonies, Communists led the fight for nationhood, while capitalism made common cause with imperialism. Communists spearheaded independence struggles in Dutch-controlled Indonesia, British Malaysia, French Indochina (including future Vietnam, Laos, and Cambodia), and the Philippines, a U.S. colony until 1946. Colonial subjects, having experienced the worst aspects of capitalism, had no special reason to believe in the power of private enterprise to bring about development. Indeed, many saw modern capitalism as itself a foreign import, the unpleasant companion of missionaries, plantation owners, gunboats, and arrogant colonial officials.

European empires unraveled swiftly in the postwar years, and dozens of new independent nations came into existence between 1945 and 1965. For the leaders of these new nations, all in the periphery and all poor, the critical issue was economic development. "Rightly or wrongly," one reporter observed about the emerging nations of the Far East, "these Asians blame their former Western rulers for the lack of development of local industry and regional trade, and their lopsided dependence on raw materials exports to uncertain Western markets."[17]

Ancient modes of production, like the hand looming of cloth by this Asian woman, represented the dead hand of the past to modernization theorists.

For them, David Engerman notes, Communism "was as much a blue-print for rapid industrialization as an ideology of proletarian rev-olution, national liberation, or totalitarian control."[18] The momentum of world communism increased markedly in 1949, when Mao Zedong finally defeated the Guomindang and took control of China. If in the 1920s Turkish intellectuals like Halidé Edib compared the United States and the Soviet Union, by the 1950s the competition between India and China captured the world's attention. "All of Asia watches the progress of . . . democratic India, comparing her development with that of Com-munist China, and drawing conclusions," a Western reporter wrote in 1955.[19]

The newly independent nations faced the same problems that earlier modernizers had: a weak central state, foreign ownership of key industries, scarcity of local capital, lack of basic infrastructure, need for imported technology, and a dearth of skilled workers, among others. In other words, the issues of modernization and eco-nomic development that we have examined in this book became the central issue of the Cold War and, arguably, the most urgent prob-lem in the second half of the 20th century and into our own time. Earlier, sovereign nations like Turkey, China, and Ethiopia sought to modernize in order to ward off the Great Powers. Now these same Great Powers hoped to strengthen the peripheral nations in order to help them ward off Communism. As the economist John Kenneth Galbraith noted, "it was accepted in the 1950s that if poor countries were not rescued from their poverty, the Communists would take over."[20] President Harry Truman accordingly urged the U.S. con-gress to increase foreign aid to help the new nations of Asia develop economically. Stability and progress, Truman insisted, could only be achieved if the United States provided "sufficient economic and technical support to enable the peoples of Asia to conquer their old deep-seated and agonizing problems, and share in the benefits of an expanding world economy."[21]

Despite Truman's upbeat message, American officials pri-vately harbored "deep fears" that Communism offered "a faster route to material well-being" for the poor in the global periphery.[22] All the new nations faced the problem of "decolonizing" their economies by reducing the dominant role of foreign companies. Some new states aligned themselves with the Soviet Union and China, nationalized foreign-owned businesses, and expropriated the private sector to become full-fledged Communist economies.

Even in non-Communist or nonaligned states, as they were called, government played a large role in directing the economy, often owning major industries outright and applying policies that favored their own citizens over foreigners.

Faced with what they saw as a worldwide drift away from capitalism, American economists and social scientists turned their attention to the "problem" of modernization. Walter W. Rostow became the best-known and most influential of these modernization theorists, as they became known. At the height of the Cold War, Rostow produced a "non-communist manifesto" spelling out how poor nations could achieve the self-sustaining growth that would lock them firmly into the capitalist world. Peripheral countries that did not make the transition to growth, Rostow warned, were at risk since Communism was a "disease" of development.

Rostow assumed that to reach modernity less-developed nations had to pass through the same historical processes as Britain and the United States, following "a single viable path to development." He believed that "all nations were merely at different points" along that path, which he schematized as four stages of economic development: "traditional, pretake-off, take-off, growing." Using data on savings and investment rates, output per capita, and other statistics, Rostow placed peripheral nations on this development timeline: Ethiopia, Kenya, Thailand, Afghanistan, and Indonesia still had "pretake-off economies," while Mexico, Chile, the Philippines, and India were "attempting take-off."[23] Industrial nations, the United States in particular, could hurry them along that timeline by applying a set of "more or less universally applicable technical interventions."[24]

Unlike European colonial officials before World War II, modernization theorists minimized the importance of racial and cultural factors in the quest for economic development. Where colonial rulers had divided the world into civilized and barbarian, the social scientists who championed modernization theory contrasted traditional with modern societies.[25] Rostow ridiculed earlier theorists who claimed the "Protestant ethic" had been essential to industrialization in the West, pointing out that "Samurai, Parsees, Jews, North Italians, [as well as] Turkish, Russian, and Chinese Civil Servants" had championed economic growth in different parts of the world. Modernization theorists like Rostow were, at root, optimistic about progress in the postcolonial world. Any society that followed their recommendations could, they said, "transform themselves in such ways that economic growth is, subsequently, more or less automatic."[26] American officials liked another optimistic strain in Rostow's theory—his assumption that countries ready to take off into self-sustaining growth did so in just a decade or two, during which period financial and technical support from the United States would prove crucial. Rostow's formula for modernization seemed to provide a plan that could defeat Communism cheaply, quickly, and peacefully.

In the late 1950s a young senator from Massachusetts preparing to run for president eagerly embraced Rostow's apparently scientific approach to modernization. John F. Kennedy made Rostow one of his key foreign policy advisers and had him prepare campaign speeches explaining how economic development could thwart Communism. In the inaugural address JFK delivered in January 1961, anxiety about the success of Communists in selling their own short-cut to modernity in the periphery is clear. "To those people in the huts and villages of half the globe struggling to break the bonds of mass misery," the new president declared, "we pledge our best efforts to help them help themselves, for whatever period is required—not because the Communists may be doing it . . . but because it is right."

To put Rostow's theories into practice, Kennedy created new programs such as Food for Peace and the Alliance for Progress in Latin America, as well as the Peace Corps, which sent young Americans into poor countries to work on development projects. Foreign aid also increased by some 30 percent under JFK. Over time, however, it became clear that modernization theorists had overstated how close many less-developed countries were to reaching the point of "take-off into self-sustaining growth" and also exaggerated how American aid could accelerate the process. As modernization stalled in many nations, armed conflict between supporters of capitalism and Communism replaced peaceful competition between the two systems. From the 1960s through the 1980s, many nations became battlegrounds—Cuba, Chile, El Salvador, Guatemala, Nicaragua, Angola, and Mozambique, among many others, in addition to Vietnam, Laos, and Cambodia. It was a sign of the times that Rostow moved away from economic modernization to become one of the main architects of the war in Vietnam under President Lyndon Johnson.

Meanwhile, anthropologists, sociologists, and other specialists working on the ground in the periphery pointed out that modernization theory largely ignored local conditions and the wishes of ordinary people. The approach obscured the diversity and complexity of peripheral societies, "so that a squatter in Mexico City, a Nepalese peasant, and a Tuareg nomad became equivalent to each other as poor and underdeveloped."[27] The one-size-fits-all approach of modernization theory recalls James Scott's observation that a "designed or planned social order is necessarily schematic; it always ignores essential features of any real, functioning social order."[28] That "schematic" approach was also reflected in the theory's assumption that as countries modernized they would become more similar, indeed more like the United States. "Modern people would all think, act, feel, and behave more or less alike."[29] Modernization was, in effect, equivalent to Americanization.

The critique of modernization proceeded on other fronts as well. In the 1960s and 1970s, historical work by Andre Gunder Frank and Emmanuel Wallerstein disputed the theory's underlying premise that all developing nations needed to follow the path blazed by early industrializers like Britain and the United States. That was impossible, Frank argued, for the simple reason that the core of industrialized nations that emerged in the 1800s had reorganized the world economy around their needs. Colonies and countries in the periphery became producers of raw materials for those countries and consumers of their finished products. Before the Industrial Revolution, Frank argued, all countries were *un*developed, but none was *under*developed. Many parts of the periphery had in fact been de-industrialized as their economic ties to the developed core nations grew stronger. In other words, "underdevelopment was and still is generated by the very same historical process which also generated economic development: the development of capitalism itself."[30] Frank's thesis, known as dependency theory, became widely popular in the 1970s, although economists argued that little hard evidence supported the argument.

MODERNIZATION OR WESTERNIZATION?

By the 1980s, modernization theory had been substantially debunked in academic circles, although a tacit version of the theory continued to direct many foreign aid programs and development projects. The theory, however, was about to get a second lease on life. On the eve of the collapse of Soviet Communism at the end of the 1980s, a vigorous new version of modernization emerged. Francis Fukuyama, a former official at the U.S. State Department, published an influential article titled "The End of History?" Fukuyama declared that the brutal conflicts of the 20th century had exhausted all serious alternatives to "economic and political liberalism," by which he meant free-market capitalism and representative democracy. The end of the Cold War, in other words, signaled the end of the ideological development of the human race and thus "the universalization of Western liberal democracy as the final form of human government."[31] Once again, it seemed, the destiny of less-developed and Communist countries was to evolve into so many versions of the United States.

Fukuyama's celebration of capitalism and democracy led the well-known political scientist Samuel Huntington to offer a pessimistic reply to all who saw post-Cold War globalization as the triumph of Americanization. Huntington, best known for his book *The Clash of Civilizations*, flatly denied that "as people in other civilizations modernize they also westernize, abandoning their traditional values, institutions and customs and adopting those that prevail in the West." To the contrary, Huntington argued, "in fundamental ways, much of the world is becoming more modern and less Western."[32]

Huntington supported this conclusion by defining modernization in essentially economic terms. As nations modernized, industrialization and urbanization allowed social mobility within new occupational structures. Social changes of course went along with economic development—higher rates of literacy and better education, among many others. Yet economic change remained distinct and separable from the embrace of Western civilization, rooted in Christianity, rule of law, pluralism, representative government, and individualism. Because of its distinctive culture, Huntington insisted, the West "was Western long before it was modern."[33]

The corollary of this idea was that other cultures could attain economic modernity without becoming Westernized, as was the case in East Asia (Japan, South Korea, Singapore, and Taiwan, among others). East Asians who had once emulated the West now believed that they had achieved economic development "because they have remained different from the West," Huntington asserted. Thus "modernization and economic development neither require nor produce cultural westernization." Indeed, as urbanization and economic growth dissolve traditions and generate feelings of alienation, modernization "creates crises of identity to which religion frequently provides an answer." Huntington thus argued that "the global revival of religion is a direct consequence of modernization."[34]

The debate about Westernization versus modernization remains open. In the harsh winter of 2008–2009, as the world financial system walked a tightrope without a net, stock markets plunged, and unemployment rates approached the levels of the Great Depression, it was all too clear that neither policy makers, academics, nor business leaders fully understood how the world economy works and what is the surest path to "self-sustaining growth." In the absence of a Cold War to make the fate of less-developed nations an urgent issue to the richest countries, there is a risk that the economic downturn will hit the poorest nations hard. A World Bank report on the crisis noted that developing countries "were being devastated by plunging exports, falling commodity prices, declining foreign investment and vanishing credit."[35] The fact that so much of the world remains so poor and vulnerable suggests that modernization is still an unfulfilled dream.

NOTES

1. Eugenio Maria de Hostos, "Civilización o Muerte," in *Paginas Dominicanas*, ed. E. Rodriguez Demorizi (Santo Domingo: Editora Taller, 1979), p. 174.

2. Quoted in Wei Li and Dennis Tao Yang, "The Great Leap Forward: Anatomy of a Central Planning Disaster," *Journal of Political Economy* 113: 4 (2005), p. 841.

3. "Say East Accepts our Machine Age," *New York Times*, August 6, 1928, p. 21.

4. Percival Spear, "Nehru," *Modern Asian Studies* 1: 1 (1967), pp. 17, 20.

5. Balkrishna Govind Gokhale, "Nehru and History," *History and Theory* 17: 3 (October 1978), p. 314.

6. Mustafa Kemal, *Speech Delivered by Ghazi Mustapha Kemal, President of the Turkish Republic, October 1927* (Leipzig: K.F. Koehler, 1929), p. 19.

7. Quoted in Arturo Escobar, *Encountering Development* (Princeton: Princeton University, 1995), p. 3.

8. "Suicides in Turkey Show an Increase," *New York Times*, 25 March 1928, p. 62.

9. "The Big Test," *New York Times*, February 24, 2009, p. A25.

10. James C. Scott, *Seeing Like a State* (New Haven: Yale, 1998), p. 5.

11. Ibid., p. 119.

12. Z. M. Fallenbuchl, "Collectivization and Economic Development," *Canadian Journal of Economics and Political Science* 33: 1 (February 1967), pp. 2, 13.

13. David C. Engerman, "Modernization from the Other Shore: American Observers and the Costs of Soviet Economic Development," *American Historical Review* 105: 2 (April 2000), p. 387.

14. Edward Beatty, *Institutions and Investment* (Stanford: Stanford University, 2001), p. 192.

15. "Say East Accepts," *New York Times*, p. 21.

16. Jawaharlal Nehru, *Toward Freedom: The Autobiography of Jawaharlal Nehru* (New York: John Day, 1941), pp. 228–230.

17. "U.S. Now Reappraising Its Policies Toward Free Asia," *New York Times*, May 8, 1955, p. E4.

18. Engerman, "Modernization," pp. 383–384.

19. "U.S. Now Reappraising Its Policies Toward Free Asia," *New York Times*, May 8, 1955, p. E4.

20. Mark H. Haefele, "Walt Rostow's Stages of Economic Growth: Ideas and Action," in Engerman et al., *Staging Growth* (Boston: University of Massachusetts, 2003), p. 84.

21. "American Aid Programme," *Times* (London), March 7, 1952, p. 5.

22. Haefele, "Walt Rostow's Stages of Economic Growth," p. 84.

23. W. W. Rostow, "The Take-Off Into Self-Sustained Growth," *Economic Journal* 66: 261 (March 1956), pp. 31, 36.

24. Escobar, *Encountering Development*, p. 44.

25. See Michael Adas, "Modernization Theory and the American Revival of the Scientific and Technological Standards of Social Achievement and Human Worth," in Engerman et al., *Staging Growth* (Boston: University of Massachusetts, 2003), pp. 35–37.

26. Rostow, "The Take-Off," pp. 25, 42.

27. Escobar, *Encountering Development*, p. 53.

28. Scott, *Seeing Like a State*, p. 6.

29. Nils Gilman, "Modernization Theory, the Highest Stage of American Intellectual History," in Engerman et al., *Staging Growth*, p. 50.

30. Andre Gunder Frank, "The Development of Underdevelopment," *Monthly Review* 18: 4 (1966), pp. 17–31.

31. Francis Fukuyama, "The End of History?" *National Interest* (Summer 1989), pp. 3, 4.

32. Samuel P. Huntington, "The West: Unique, Not Universal," *Foreign Affairs*, November–December 1996, pp. 28, 38.

33. Ibid., pp. 29–30.

34. Ibid., pp. 37–38.

35. "World Bank Says Global Economy Will Shrink in '09," *New York Times*, March 9, 2009, p. B1.

Bibliography

GENERAL WORKS

The introduction touches on a host of topics, and each has a significant literature. The suggestions that follow thus point out several important texts on each theme that should be available in most college or larger public libraries as well as for purchase through the Internet. On the Industrial Revolution and the economic impact of technology, see Robert C. Allen, *The British Industrial Revolution in Global Perspective* (2009); Douglass C. North, *Structure and Change in Economic History* (1981); David S. Landes, *The Unbound Prometheus: Technological Change and Industrial Development in Western Europe, 1750 to the Present* (1969); and Joel Mokyr, *The Lever of Riches: Technological Creativity and Economic Progress* (1992).

On nationalism, the modern classic is Benedict Anderson, *Imagined Communities: Reflections on the Origin and Spread of Nationalism* (2006). Other important works include Ernest Gellner, *Nations and Nationalism* (2009) and E. J. Hobsbawm and Terence Ranger, eds., *The Invention of Tradition* (1992), a well-known collection of iconoclastic essays.

On the rise of the West to world domination, see William McNeil, *The Pursuit of Power: Technology, Armed Force and Power since 1000 A.D.* (1984); Charles Tilly, *Coercion, Capital and European States, AD 990–1992* (1992); and Immanuel Wallerstein, *The Modern World-System III: The Second Era of Great Expansion of the Capitalist World-Economy, 1730–1840s* (1989). On the impact of Western power in the periphery, see Michael Adas, *Machines as the Measure of Men: Science, Technology and Ideologies of Western Domination* (1990) and Daniel R. Headrick, *Tools of Empire: Technology and European Imperialism in the Nineteenth Century* (1981).

Several works take up the central issue of *Great Leaps Forward* but offer more theoretical studies of defensive modernization in less-developed states. A classic study by a political scientist is Ellen Kay Trimberger, *Revolution from Above: Military Bureaucrats and Development in Turkey, Egypt, Japan and Peru* (1978). A more recent work, also from a political science perspective, is Atul Kohli's *State-Directed Development: Political Power and Industrialization in the Global Periphery* (2004), which examines how state policies promoted industrialization and economic growth in Brazil, India, Nigeria, and South Korea. Another study of the drive for economic development since World War II is Alice H. Amsden's *The Rise of "The Rest": Challenges to the West from Late-Industrializing Economies* (2003), which like Kohli's work looks at the policies that allowed some postwar states to industrialize successfully while others failed to do so. Philip D. Curtin, a leading historian of Africa and European imperialism, examines the manifold ways that Africans, indigenous Americans, and Asians reacted to Western power in *The World and the West: The European Challenge and the Overseas Response in the Age of Empire* (2002).

The encounter of modern and premodern societies is captured by fiction and film as well as historical studies. Novels such as E. M. Forster's *Passage to India*, Joseph Conrad's *Heart of Darkness*, and Rudyard Kipling's *Kim*, among many others, all unfold in territories of the British Empire. Evelyn Waugh offers a cynical view of a European-educated African modernizer and his foreign hangers-on in *Black Mischief*, first published in 1932. African views of European colonialism are presented by Chinua Achebe in *Things Fall Apart*, first published in 1958, and in Ngũgĩ wa Thiong'o's *Weep Not, Child*, a fictional account of conditions in Kenya leading to the Mau Mau rebellion against British rule, originally published in 1964. Both are available in modern editions. A chilling fictional account of early U.S. efforts to promote modernization as an alternative to both Communism and colonialism is Graham Greene's *Quiet American* (2004), published in 1955, long before most Americans had heard of Vietnam. Senegalese filmmaker Sembène Ousmane's acclaimed film *The Camp at Thiaroye* (1987), based on real events in which soldiers from West Africa rebelled against French colonial rule, is filled with discussion of the contradictory impact of "Western civilization" on Africa.

MEXICO

The best single-volume study of Díaz, providing not only a detailed biography but also surveying the changing views of historians since the 19th century, is Paul Garner's *Porfirio Díaz* (2001). William H. Beezley provides a fascinating study of the leisure culture of Mexico's upper class during the Porfiriato in *Judas at the Jockey Club and Other Episodes of Porfirian Mexico* (2004). The other end of Mexico's social scale is explored in Paul Vanderwood's highly readable *Disorder and Progress: Bandits, Police and Mexican Development* (1981), which focuses on the "pacification" of Mexico during the Porfiriato.

Important recent works on economic modernization that stress the achievements of the Díaz regime include Stephen Haber, *Industry and Underdevelopment: The Industrialization of Mexico, 1890–1940* (1989) and Edward Beatty, *Institutions and Investment: The Political Basis of Industrialization in Mexico Before 1911* (2001). For contrasting views of modernization and its effects, see E. Bradford Burns, *The Poverty of Progress: Latin America in the Nineteenth Century* (1983), a general study of modernization in Latin America, and Jeffrey Bortz and Stephen Haber, eds., *The Mexican Economy, 1870–1930* (2001).